Original Fire:

THE Hidden Heart of Religious Women

Brenda Peddigrew, RSM, Ph.D.

Introduction by Diarmuid O'Murchu

Endorsements For Original Fire

Providing the kindling for life-changing conversations, this is a book to be passed from hand to hand among those living in spiritual community. With the dedication and passion of a contemporary Hildegard of Bingen or Theresa of Avila, Sister Brenda's astute analysis of the past and fiery commitment to ongoing transformation will profoundly shift the way you think about religious life and communal commitment. She deeply trusts our future and offers a possible way.

– Sister Gabriele Uhlein, Past-President of the Franciscan Federation and author of *Meditations with Hildegard of Bingen*

The lives of women religious deserve the exploratory honoring that Sr. Brenda Peddigrew provides in Original Fire. Peddigrew's scholarship is a contribution to the contextual understanding of women within the Roman Catholic Church and will also appeal to a wider womanist readership, Anyone who values stories of lineage and liberation will be moved by this look into the hearts and minds of women religious.

– Christina Baldwin, author of *Storycatcher, The Seven Whispers, Life's Companion,* and *Calling the Circle.*

I have waited a long time for this book. Running with the flow of history in our own time, Brenda Peddigrew traces the story of ten fiery women in contemporary religious life. These women exhibit in our time the subverted tradition of times past. By accessing their stories through the investigative tools of Organic Inquiry, we access the deep dreams, yearnings, struggles and hopes that characterize prophetic religious woman down through history.

– Diarmuid O'Murchu (from his introduction), author of *Religious Life: A Prophetic Vision(1991); Reframing Religious Life(1998); Poverty, celibacy and Obedience(1999); Consecrated Religious Life(2005)*

iii

Dedication

*to all Catholic Vowed Women, past and present, who were
first my teachers, then sisters, mentors, colleagues, friends,
and finally companions on the terrible beautiful path of
transformation that we continue to walk...and especially to*

the Sisters of Mercy of Newfoundland and Labrador, Canada

TABLE OF CONTENTS

INTRODUCTION

I have waited a long time for this book. As a young religious in the 1970s, I scoured the history of religious life, striving to make sense of the confusion I felt amid the new waves of change that were emerging at that time. And history came to my rescue with abundant and inspiring examples of breakthrough and fresh hope.

I was inspired by outstanding heroes like Anthony of Egypt, Benedict, Francis, Ignatius, Vincent de Paul and the several founders of 18th. century France. The relative absence of great foundresses had somehow eluded me. Even when for the first time I read about Angela Merici, foundress of the Ursuline Sisters (in Lawrence Cada & Alia, Shaping the Coming Age of Religious Life, NY:Seabury Press, 1979), it did not register with me that foundresses promoted a model of Religious Life very different from their male counterparts. Only upon reading the monumental work of Jo Ann Kay McNamara (*Sisters in Arms*, Cambridge, MA: Harvard University Press, 1996), did the fuller truth penetrate my well formed masculine intellect.

Women as counter-cultural

In the Introduction to *Sisters in Arms,* Jo Ann describes the Virgins of the early church not merely as women of outstanding virtue and holiness (the conventional interpretation) but as counter-cultural women who opted for a life of virginity in protest against a patriarchal culture where a woman could only achieve status as a man's wife or mother. The Virgins proclaimed a new freedom and vision of woman as a person in her own right, irrespective of the assigned roles of the dominant society. I have never come across a Church history manual that acknowledges this fact.

Thus begins the long story of female religious life in the Christian church, a story still waiting to be told in the clear light of justice and truth. Women have always outnumbered men in the vowed life. Yet, history tilts the scales heavily in favour of the males.Church history manuals exonerate the great founders and pay scant attention to the great foundresses; in several historical works, the foundresses are not even mentioned. The distinctive female contribution has been subverted and often made invisible.

Visionaries who paid the price

And understandably so in the face of the dominant culture. Women do things differently even in their witness to the vowed life. And the great foundresses offer a distinctively alternative model of evangelical witness. They bring passion and radical vision to reading the signs of the times, and in their desire to contribute to the building up of God's kingdom on earth they dream new horizons far in excess of the ecclesiastical constrictions of the time.

Joan Chittister vividly captivates the truth of female religious life when she writes: "Hagiography, folklore and the archives of religious congregations are full of the stories of strong-minded women who challenged bishops and bested them, confronted popes and chastised them, contested the norms of the society and corrected them." (The Fire in these ashes, Kansas City: Sheed & Ward 1995, 12). As Brenda Peddigrew indicates in her opening chapters, many of the foundresses openly confronted and challenged church authority incurring ridicule, marginalisation, intense suffering at times and, not in a few cases, censure to the point of excommunication.

Christian religious life can never hope to reclaim its prophetic grandeur until this historical anomaly is righted and the true story illuminates our way in the service of God and humanity. Reclaiming our history will not be easy. Sadly, the suppression of the feminine still prevails in contemporary religion. Much more serious is the struggle to reclaim the past when so much of the evidence has been subverted, made invisible and even destroyed.

Reclaiming Subverted Stories

This is where Brenda Peddigrew's Original Fire becomes a work of enormous impact. What we cannot access from our deep past can also be recovered from our creative present. Liminal women, who stand courageously at the cutting edge with fiery vision and undaunting hope have characterised religious life at every moment in history. Joan Chittister highlights the underlying dream when she writes: "Of all the issues facing religious life, feminism is surely the most veiled and the most dangerous because it brings us most in conflict with the flow of history." (The Fire in These Ashes,166).

Running with the flow of history in our own time, Brenda Peddigrew traces the story of ten fiery women in contemporary religious life. These women exhibit in our time the subverted tradition of times past. By accessing their stories through the investigative tools of Organic Inquiry, we access the deep dreams, yearnings, struggles and hopes that characterise the prophetic religious woman down through history.

The benefits of such exploration are numerous. Most importantly, for me at least, is the historical sense of justice being reclaimed so that we can honour the full story of the vowed life in the Christian tradition. In doing so, we become painfully aware of the many other fiery women (and men) who have left religious congregations because the internal climate was alien to their fiery giftedness. Fortunately, a number of those same women are reconnected through associate programmes, especially in Western countries.

As we look to the future

And for the future of religious life, this enlarged and inclusive historical narrative will offer much needed wisdom and hope. Religious Life today is in decline and will remain so for some time to come. With the diminishment of the former paradigm, already the seeds of new life are beginning to sprout. As on all previous life-cycles, female foundations are likely to prove the most daring and innovative. Perhaps, we glimpse something of that new vision in the individual stories narrated in this book.

But Original Fire is not just for female religious although clearly they are the primary focus. It also carries inspiration and hope all of us – women and men – who struggle to honour the liminal and prophetic horizons of the vowed life. The liminal cutting age can be an exciting space but at times a very lonely place to be. Original Fire depicts a landscape where even in the depths of our loneliness, we know we are not alone. Many kindred spirits share our dreams and it is encouraging to know that we are befriended by a community of liminal ancestors in the great women and men of history.

And as for history itself, it is also reassuring to know that Her-story is reclaiming its legitimate place along His-story. One hopes that Original Fire is just the first of many more such books that truly honours the wisdom that has been subverted for far too long.

Diarmuid O'Murchu MSC

CHAPTER I:

Fiery Foundresses: These Are the Women We Come From

Margaret Aylward, foundress of the Ladies of Charity of St. Vincent dePaul in Dublin, who was imprisoned for six months.

Mary McKillop, foundress of the Sisters of St. Joseph in Australia, who was excommunicated for insubordination to the Bishop of her Diocese.

Catherine McAuley, who didn't want to found a religious congregation because of the enclosed state of religious women of her time, later capitulated from Diocesan pressure, but became an object of the Bishop's personal vendetta because she applied to the Pope, not to him.

Cornelia Connelly, foundress of the Sisters of the Holy Child Jesus, who pursued her dream through the deaths of her children, the defection of her husband into the priesthood, then his defection out of it, pressuring her to return to the marriage.

Mary Aikenhead, foundress of the Irish Sisters of Charity, who was chosen "against her will" by Archbishop Murray, coadjutor of Dublin, "to carry out his plan of rounding a Congregation of the Sisters of Charity in Ireland."

1

Nano Nagle, foundress of the Presentation Sisters, who broke the English Penal Laws and rejected the strict rules of the Ursulines in order to educate Catholic children.

Margaret Cusack, foundress of the Sisters of St. Joseph of Peace, who so publicly supported women's suffrage that the Vatican ordered her name removed as foundress of her community.

Mary Ward, foundress of the Loretto Sisters, who saw the role of women in the Church as equal to that of Jesuit priests, and thus the order was suppressed by Pius V.

This list could be much longer. Too often, when we celebrate the public stories of women who founded religious communities, we emphasize their miraculous achievement, their strength and steadfastness, their devotion and faith. All of this is true. But the whole story includes their difficulties and struggles, their opposition from Church and State – mostly because they were women – and the tremendous obstacles they overcame to make their vision real in the world. Omitting the stories of struggle diminishes the power of these women, and especially diminishes their significance for our inspiration today.

Seeing what is not present

The foundresses were women who lived the ordinary life of their ordinary time. They suffered from the same complaints, the same seductions, the same limits as we suffer from in ours. They saw visions – as we see visions, were we to pay attention to them, to trust them – and they made the visions happen. They made the invisible, visible. To accomplish this, they believed in their vision to such a degree that they allowed no obstacle to obfuscate their clarity, be it Church, state or cultural conditioning.

The gift of their vision was *seeing very concretely what was not there, what was not yet present but was needed in their own cultures*. For Catherine McAuley, it was the education of poor women, and visiting the sick poor in their homes. Educating poor women - something unheard of in her times – is a common thread among many foundresses: Mary McKillop in Australia, Margaret Cusack, Nano Nagle, Mary Ward – they and many others clearly and with consequences blatantly went against the standards of their time regarding how women were perceived and treated.

Another distinguishing feature of foundresses is their common focus on service of and advocacy for the socially deprived. Although foundresses belonged to Christian denominations, mainly Roman Catholic, they did not bring their followers together to serve the Church, but people. From the beginning, this distinction must be noted: that although the founding work was grounded and inspired in faith and spiritual devotion, the original vision was not to serve an institutional Church, but the ordinary needs of people whom the Church – as well as the state – was neglecting. From this reality comes the consistent, evident conflict that many – even most – foundresses experienced with Church officials from their beginnings and the reason why they are poorly treated in Church history books: often they are deprived of their humanity and made into bloodless saints. It was only after the communities were actually formed that foundresses became increasingly subject to Church restrictions, and usually after the death of the foundress and founding members. Slowly, priorities changed from serving the original vision to serving the Church, which was not at all the same thing, and contributes even today to a lessening of the transforming power that was present in the first visions of foundresses.

During the past forty years, as the clerical Church declines in numbers and influence in the developed world, Catholic vowed women have taken on pastoral and some restricted liturgical roles that were formerly exclusive to male priests, though they continue to be denied the equality of ordination attained by women in other Christian denominations. Some Catholic vowed women are in the forefront of the struggle for equality within the Roman Catholic Church, but not as many as one might think, given the long history of subservience and control demanded by and given to the Vatican. A small number of women in most Congregations – though they are by far a minority – are beginning to include the Church, along with the more traditional target of a materialistic society – as an unjust structure to be opposed.

Original Fire

Thus continues the thread of prophetic tradition that has distinguished vowed religious women from the beginning. They all lived that founding moment in their lives from the place of what I am calling here "original fire" – that personal, interior shift from a life of conforming to outer authority to claiming an inner authority powerful enough to not only bring about a reality that didn't exist before, but to fight heaven and earth, to be the target of personal insult and outright opposition, to do so.

When we who are their descendants benefit from their strong vision, we are deceiving ourselves if we believe that the same is not asked of us. Where we are now is similar to the current lament of feminists who point out how the younger women of today who didn't endure the struggle for women's equality have no idea of the costs to women's lives that have been paid for decades, just so they can experience the freedom they so take for granted today. Similarly, when we neglect to remind ourselves of that original vision and how it can be applied today, and simply give ourselves over to the comfort and security of the structure that has evolved from that vision, we betray something profound, both within our single selves and within the communities we have been given, deserving the stereotypical caricatures assigned us by media and movies.

Loss of liminality

Where has that strong, vision-driven spirit of the foundresses gone? What has drained us of our fire, that fire so crucial to what drew us together in the first place? O'Murchu (1999) posits an answer:

> The major crisis facing the vowed life today is that it has largely lost touch with its capacity to serve in a liminal capacity. It has been largely domesticated and excessively institutionalized, not merely in religious (ecclesiastical) terms, but also because it has over identified with the conventional behaviours of secular life. Religious tend to work and minister in institutions sponsored by state or church, sometimes by both. Such involvement hinders the ability to act in a liminal and prophetic way. (19)

When we remember how women founded the active, service-oriented Congregations that flourished for a hundred and fifty years and more, what leaps out is their confident determination to bypass the institutions of their time – Church, government, even law - to break through into a larger light. They acted from liminal power, they dared prophetic action and took the cost of that – an intimate personal cost of illness and early death, in many cases – as part of their calling to change their world for the better.

Who of us lives from liminal power today? Which of our communities chooses the power of the "threshold experience... those places apart where we are invited to provide a mirror-image in which people can see reflected their own searchings, struggles and hopes for a more meaningful existence...God, working through the people, creates liminal spaces."(O'Murchu, 1999, 12) Liminal living, from which emerges prophetic seeing and speaking, can well be equated with that spirit to whom Jesus referred when he said "the spirit blows where it wills. You cannot tell where it comes from or where it is going." (John 11:21) How is it possible to contain such spirit in an institution or any organization whose major energy and resources go into solidifying structure and security, making the future safe, or guaranteeing conformity to teachings and policies?

No, the liminal spirit of foundresses does not live in such organizations, but in the hearts of individuals who have not given their souls over to the organization, even if they still belong. And many don't – yet they are no less liminal and prophetic for having stepped outside it.

Questions that might now be asked

How did the religious life of women become so primarily defined in theological, ecclesiastical, anthropological or even sociological terms? What happened to the vital individual personalities of the early women, the conflicts and reconciliations, the power of the common work that kept it all going, the deep faith lived so personally and tenderly?

Who are we as women among women, as human beings struggling with other human beings? Who are we without canonical and religious trappings, and when we speak the simple truth of human experience without spiritualizing it out of all recognition? What is the daily understory of lives so distinctly circumscribed by the male religious authority of the Roman Catholic hierarchy?

I realize as I write that many vowed women will not identify with these questions. Perhaps they have been indoctrinated in an ecclesiastical cult of "right answers" rather than "right

6

questions." This situation is little different from that of married women who are faithful to the institution of marriage because it is law or sacrament, neglecting their own lives to make husband and children happy. Some would say that this situation no longer exists, but I would protest – and illustrate – otherwise.

Feminists, notwithstanding

Personal experience has been generally excluded from the public identification of Catholic vowed women; we are not seen with individual talents and voices, but as "nuns," that impersonal group identity. In allowing this, we have diminished, not enhanced, our collective power for good. Bergeron (2002,16) asks "How can religious life remain faithful to its own being and mission if it disassociates itself from feminism when understood as a quest for the emancipation of all humanity?" A basic tenet of feminism (Oleson, 1994, 164) is the principle that "the personal is the political" and that therefore women's stories are themselves the grounds for that emancipation. In gathering the material for this study, it became clear to me that a very large gap exists between the declared association of many vowed women's communities with feminist principles and the actual living out of those principles, and that gap consists of the lack of value given to the life experience – in a communal way – of individual members. Kate, one of the storytellers in a later chapter, and a former provincial (leader) of her community, puts it succinctly: "we'd been using feminist language, but the structures aren't feminist."

Although the word "feminist" was unheard of in their times, many foundresses would readily be deemed so by today's standards. Some might even be referred to as "radical feminists," a derogatory word in many quarters today. Mary McKillop would not relinquish her value of an egalitarian community rather than a hierarchical one. Catherine McAuley so refused to comply with cultural expectations of women that a Dublin clergymen addressed mail to her as "Catherine McAuley, esq." a sarcastic expression of his perception that she had overstepped her feminine boundaries and was acting inappropriately as a man. Nano Nagle openly practiced civil disobedience and Margaret Cusack so blatantly supported women's suffrage that the Vatican condemned her publicly and removed her name as foundress of her order. Mary Ward saw no reason why her women had to be enclosed, nor why they had to be subject to Bishops. "Women ruling women" and the freedom to travel alone were so radical for her time that her beginning organization was suppressed by Rome.

In a subsequent chapter we will explore in more detail the noteworthy fact that the difficulties encountered by the strong, visionary women who addressed unjust social circumstances in their historical moments came mainly from the Church itself, often in the form of local clergymen. There are fewer reports of opposition arising from government officials, or any other organized body.

At this moment in our history, it is worth noting yet again, and hopefully through a different lens, the ability of foundresses to withstand formidable and personal opposition. In our time, the groups of women who for centuries have followed the values of their foundresses in an organizational way are dying. The factors contributing to their demise are complex and inseparable from the conditions of rapid change affecting the whole of the planet. Yet, in an age when women have more freedom than at any other time in history, at least in the developed world, is it not ironic that there is so little evidence of the fiery, single-minded visions of our foundresses, translated into what is needed in today's world? As organizations, we have lost that original fire. We have become overly Church-focused and compliant to a structure that has no value for us except in that compliance, a Church that turns its back on faithful questioning, pastoral contemplation, and focusing on people rather than pope. We collude – as Congregations – with a structure that wants women only as servants – and not with any spiritual meaning in that word.

This statement is generally true of religious orders of women as organizations trying to stay within Canon Law, but it is not true of some of their individual members. The stories you will find in chapters IV and V attest to this fallacy well and fully. Because we have not found a way to encourage and value individual voices, they have not found an effective place within our organizational structures.

While what I write here may sound at first and to some hopeless and negative, this is not my intention nor is it the reality that is visible to me. What I see among the visible ruins is the invisible light, the thread of transformation carried forward in a way particular to those who have lived in women's religious communities during the past forty to sixty years. The transformation taking place is indeed hidden, but in the way of seeds moving naturally into dormancy as a phase of passing into another, more visible form. The intense dedication and compassionate service of generations of vowed women will not be lost. Even those who lived for a few (or many) years among us, whose spirits called them elsewhere – they too continue to carry the seeds of faith and hope that echo our own. The legalities of Canon Law do not apply to spirit.

Future unfolding

As structures fall into ruins, as buildings are sold and property carefully negotiated with developers to preserve our values as much as possible, as the life itself is not only not questioned but dismissed as viable by young people who would, in former ages, carry it onward, what is still happening? I ask the question not in the outer sense of works and ministries, but in the inner sense of the nature of the transformation that parallels the outer stripping away that is no longer deniable. How does what is happening relate to the original fire of the women with whom this chapter began?

Collecting stories for this study led to one clear theme, and this theme is the surprising bridge that exists between Catholic vowed women and women everywhere, women who have had no experience- and in some cases no knowledge – of religious life. The theme is this – and it is congruent with the foundresses who must have made this shift themselves: *women who live within oppressive structures, whether male or female-dominant, by following their natural individuation process, shift from conforming to outer authority to recognizing and acting on their inner authority*. When these two are in conflict, a significant number of women will find a way, however small, to live from their inner authority, even while appearing to conform to the outer one. Indeed, this latter strategy has been by far the safest for many women. The struggle to keep alive personal, purposeful vitality – original fire – in the daily presence of oppressive and unfeeling authority structures echoes a more general experience of women caught in analogous cultural demands, be they marriage or work-related. Responses of several women who have never known vowed life from the inside are offered in chapter VIII, validating this connection.

Soul of this work

The soul of this book is the telling of eleven stories, deeply personal and also woven into the structures I have been naming here. These stories articulate a deeply personal struggle to keep alive each one's original fire against a backdrop of historical denigration of women by Western culture in general and the Roman Catholic Church in particular, both as women and as members of canonically vowed communities. Even the renewal of communities, opened up by Vatican Council II in 1965, was mandated: it didn't arise from within the communities themselves. But it opened a space- the nature of which was perhaps not originally intended - and allowed energies to move that were obviously ready to do so. Now, after 40 years of renewal, of planning, legalizing and strategizing, "renewal" has taken us as far as it can. We stand on the doorstep of transformation, and it is a place that our foundresses – the women we come from – would understand very well.

CHAPTER II:

When It All Changed: "Return to the Founding Spirit"

To acknowledge our ancestors means we are aware
that we did not make ourselves
that the line stretches all the way back, perhaps to God...
We remember then because it is an easy thing to forget:
that we are not the first to suffer, rebel, fight, love and ie.
The grace with which we embrace life,
in spite of the pain, the sorrows,
is always a measure of what has gone before."
(Alice Walker, quoted in Welch, 1990, 21)

What was this Vatican Council II, and why was it so significant in the lives of Catholics? No one really expected the election of Pope John XXIII in the first place, a man generally deemed "too old" for the position; his convoking of a General Council was even more unexpected. But his words at the Council's opening gave many Catholics a kind of bright hope that they'd seldom heard from the guilt-and-sin focused Church:

> For with the opening of this Council a new day is dawning
> on the Church, bathing her heart in radiant splendor. It is
> yet the dawn, but the sun in its rising has already set our

hearts aglow. All around is the fragrance of holiness and joy (John XXIII, 1963).

His poetic words gave hope and courage to Catholics everywhere; still, the renewal was mandated, and that is the key word here. In the document "Perfectae Caritatis" (Vatican II, 1965), the document written especially for vowed religious men and women, Congregations were told to return to the "spirit of their founding" and to reclaim their "original charism," or founding spirit —within Canon Law, of course. The first layer of obeying this Vatican mandate was the shedding of external restrictions. The question of whether or not the women wanted to do so was—as far as I can tell—never considered, yet they worked away at obeying the church's mandate for the past 40 years. Some will say that change was fermenting from within and the mandate simply opened the possibility for it to happen, but I wonder what would really have happened if Catholic vowed women had been given a choice in 1965.

The significance of Vatican Council II for the lives of religious women's Congregations can hardly be imagined by those who did not live it. Ending in 1965, and including in its documents "Perfectae Caritatis", the "Decree on the Up-To-Date Renewal of Religious Life", Vatican II – as it came to be called – opened not only windows, but doors for experimenting with change in the way vowed women lived. The title of a popular book at the time, "Vows But No Walls," captured the growing spirit of this moment in history.

"Walled" is what Catholic vowed women had become, and it was a long way from the spirit of freedom and daring embodied in the foundresses. Over the decades, even the active Congregations had been pulled into the monastic mode of strict horariums and more silence than speaking. Containment in structure, finalized by the inclusion of religious women in the code of Canon Law in 1921, effectively brought the lives of vowed women into and under the control of the Church, to the extent that – aside from teaching and nursing in Congregational institutions approved by the Church – nuns were seldom encountered as human beings, not to mention as women.. The fiery spirits of the founding members could no longer be seen.

In order to glimpse how and why this might have come about, two contextual reflections might be helpful here.

- We will look directly at the role of the Roman Catholic Church in the lives of Catholic vowed women, focusing on a history of misogyny, domination and abuse; a history that if often hinted at but not highlighted;

- We will examine the long silence of Catholic vowed women and how this silence reflects the general silence of women in Western culture;

The Role of the Roman Catholic Church

Throughout centuries, the Roman Catholic Church has operated from a fixed belief of the world as an apprehendable reality. This applies not only to the material world we see, but about the next as well. Heaven and Hell, and what was going on in them, as well as who is going there, was as secure a certainty as an answer from the first-grade Baltimore Catechism: "God made me to know, love and serve him in this world so that I can be happy with him in the next." (U.S. Bishops, 1891/1921, 7) Brueggemann sees this very certainty as the greatest threat to the Church when he says: "I regard relativisim as less of a threat than objectivism, which I believe to be a very large threat among us precisely because it is such a deception" (Brueggemann, 1993, cited in O'Murchu, 2000, 10).

Even today, standing desperately against a postmodernist world in which certainty is perceived as death-dealing rather than life-giving, it is evident that this Church has not departed from its belief in the possibility of objectivity within a dualistic worldview as a primary way to live and teach. (Congregation for the Doctrine of the Faith, 2000) It is the positivist paradigm that continues the absolute rule of hierarchical authority, papal infallibility, the silencing of dissenting thinkers, and the refusal—under pain of job loss in Catholic institutions—to allow discussion of women's ordination or to question Church policy on homosexuality. Jeannine Grammick (Schaeffer, 2000) and Carmel MacEnroe (Murphy, 1997) suffered the results of defying such Vatican mandates, the first by being publicly silenced because of her work with Catholic homosexuals; the second fired from her professorship at a Catholic university for allowing the topic of the ordination of women to be discussed in her classroom.

The consciousness of such a Church is described succinctly in a rather long quote (Marion, 2000) that I nevertheless offer here:

At the mythic level of consciousness the child is "good" if the child follows the rules and "bad" if it breaks them. The child learns to see his or her own intense self-worth in terms of these external rules and roles, and in terms of pleasing these external gods...for the adult Christian who has not progressed beyond the mythic level, it is important to convert the whole world to the one true Christian religion (and to make sure that governments enact laws that agree with what the believer has been taught are "Christian" morals)...this requires the elimination, by conversion or otherwise, of all "others" because they are seen as threatening the believers' externally defined sense of worth...it is alright to impose one's belief system on others, and to punish those who believe otherwise. After all, it is for the others' own good that they submit to the "truth" as the mythic believer assumes the truth to be (43).

The emphasis on conforming to external beliefs as a measuring stick of who does or does not belong still characterizes the Vatican Church today. O'Murchu (2000) raises this questionable right of who decides who belongs when he says

> the spiritual seeker may be confronted with the choice of being in the Church or outside it. This is yet another dualism often used to label and categorize people, a subtle and devious way of exerting control over people's lives. It is a classical patriarchal ploy that needs to be exposed and denounced. As creatures of the universe and inhabitants of planet Earth, there are, in the eyes of God, no reserved places (17).

The history of the Christian Church, even in the gospels, rings with conflict and opposition, ambivalence and ambiguity. (Neander, 1993; Pagels,1979, pp.xi-xxix; Waite, 1992)

Jesus asked his apostles, "who do you say that I am?" (Matthew 16:15) after hearing some of the conflicting rumours; even his followers were not in agreement while he was alive. (Brown, Fitzmyer and Murphy, 1990, 349) The ambition of some of the apostles to "sit on his right and left hand in the Kingdom" (Matthew 12:42) exasperated Jesus as they continued to apply his teachings to a material instead of a spiritual world. After his death, the conflict between Peter and Paul divided the new church (Galatians 2:14), and this thread of conflict can be traced throughout the entire history of Christianity. (Bossy, 1985; Evans & Unger, 1992; Hillgarth, 1969; Hoare, 1965). A turning point for this oppositional ambience was the Edict of Milan in 325 C.E. (Pagels,1979, xxiv), when the Roman Emperor Constantine decreed Christianity to be the official religion of the

Empire. With this declaration, the decision to become Christian shifted from an inner, private one to an outer, public one. One of Constantine's first acts was to make baptism mandatory, and thousands upon thousands were baptized as a matter of form. The publicizing of Christianity brought it into the realm of politics and power (Kung, 2003, 23), a characteristic that found many forms in its two thousand years of history (Aarons & Loftus, 1998; Kung, 2003; Martin, 1981; Wills, 2001). The Roman Church's predilection for power and wealth is heavily documented; along with the sources just quoted, Fox (1983; 1994); Starhawk (1996) add additional voices to the research.

Duplicity of every kind can be traced throughout the whole of that history. Brown and Bohn (1989), Williams (1991) and Bailie (2001), the last two authors interpreting René Girard, endeavor to identify the violence inherent in Biblical texts and to rescue Christianity from association with that violence, but their success is hidden from all but the academic few as we daily watch the most powerful leaders in the Western world calling on the Christian God to bless and sanction their plans for war.

What is readily evident in a historical review is that many Church leaders quickly began to act as hypocritically as the Pharisees whom Jesus loudly and consistently condemned in his public ministry. (Matthew 13-36; Luke 11:39-44) One of the most significant areas in which this appears to be true and which is being so vividly publicized in our time is that of sexual behavior. While teaching one ideal of "purity," especially for clergy, for whom celibacy is mandatory, we are now seeing, through authors such as Kennedy (2002); Grant (1994); Sipe (1998); Cozzens (2000, 2002), Rossetti (1990), Jordan (2000) and the Winter Commission Report (1990), as well as the Boston Globe Investigative Staff (2002), that significant numbers of clergy are not only sexually active, both heterosexually and homosexually, but that they contain among their numbers pedophiles and abusers of every persuasion.

The Church's historical relationship to women needs to be seen in the context of this general history of conflict and duplicitous teaching.

Women's Place in the Roman Church

The relationship of the Church to women, and especially to vowed women, reflects a long, controlling history. Women's response to this control shows a definite thread of defiance; that is, questioning and finding ways to act outside the norm is noticeable in story after recorded story. (McNamara, 1996). Most communities of vowed women came into being because their founders went against the established norms of their times, which McNamara shows in great detail. A few fine examples of the fiery spirit of resistance and creative contribution to social needs by foundresses of religious communities of women clearly continue this historical thread, begun in Chapter 1. **Angela Merici** (1474-1540) of Desenzano, Italy, founder of the Ursuline Order, formed her women "without distinctive habit, without solemn vows and enclosure" (Catholic Information Network 2003), which was directly counter to the prevailing notions of her time. Indeed, at the age of 56, she deliberately refused Pope Clement IV's request to formalize her association of women into a religious order: Her association of women educators—known today as the Ursulines—only became so after her lifetime. They became the first group of religious women to work outside the cloister and the first association of teaching women, but only because Angela refused to conform to the papal and clerical demands of her time. Soon after Angela's death, **Mary Ward** (1585-1645) of Yorkshire, England, founded a community of active sisters in 1609 to educate young women, spread the faith in places where priests could not go, and give aid to persecuted Catholics. For this vision, Mary Ward was "criticized and vilified for her efforts to expand the role of women religious in spreading the faith, imprisoned by Church officials who called her a dangerous heretic" (Institute of the Blessed Virgin Mary, 2003). Her work was destroyed and her sisters had to go into hiding from clerical enemies; nevertheless, she continued "to live her fidelity to God with cheerfulness and a passion for truth" (Institute of the Blessed Virgin Mary, 2003), nurturing her concept of groups of women with no enclosure, habit, or rule by men. Today, her followers are called "Loretto Sisters," and are prominent in educational fields.

In Ireland there was **Catherine McAuley** (1778-1842), who continued the same vision of an association of women educating women, and of visiting the sick poor in their homes. A wealthy Dublin socialite with an inheritance large enough to build the "House of Mercy" on Baggot Street in Dublin which still stands today (Regan & Keiss, 1988, 57). Catherine did not want her women or her works to be contained by ecclesiastical restriction. She saw enclosure as preventing good works from taking place where they are most needed and sent her women out in pairs to the poorest parts of Dublin, then all Ireland, England and the world. In the tradition of Angela and Mary, Catherine McAuley was treated by some Bishops and priests of her time with derision bordering on persecution (Healey, 1973, 76). One of these Bishops, as mentioned in Chapter 1, addressed her mail as "Catherine McAuley, Esq." (Sullivan, 1995, 123) to indicate that she didn't know her place as a woman and was acting with a man's authority. Catherine's followers, the Sisters of Mercy, eventually became the largest group of English-speaking religious women in the world, ministering on every continent (Regan & Keiss, 42).

A final example of the fiery spirit of foundresses is **Mary McKillop** (1842-1909), founder of the Sisters of St. Joseph of Australia. She came into conflict with Roman Catholic Church authorities over educational matters, and because she formed her sisters into an egalitarian rather than a hierarchical organization.

Mary McKillop was actually excommunicated from the Church in 1871 by Bishop Spiel for insubordination (Convict Creations, 2003).

Today, however, the questions are more public and the actions more direct. Schneiders (1991a) wrote—referring to the relationship of women and the Church—that "the old garment is beyond repair...no doubt such a project is frightening to those who still equate the garment of monochromatic masculinism with the unity of the Church" (vi). Fiand (1990) had just the year before laid bare the lack of systemic questioning in renewal efforts by saying that "studies dealing with our founding and with past theologies of religious life cannot be excused any longer for ignoring ecclesiastical dualism and its almost universal oppression and infantilization of women" (23). The stories of the women in this book, the "hidden heart of religious women", directly reflect the spirit of all those mentioned above, and stand directly in that historical line of fire, resisting enclosure and repression of women's knowing and action.

Of all that could be said of the Roman Catholic Church's requirement of strict adherence to its teaching authority, what is most relevant here is its continuing position on women and their role in Church and society. The history of vowed women within this tradition is marked with a traceable line of an "authentic atmosphere of terror and oppression; ultimately, Rome struggled to retain its ancient customs and its ancient social systems by ferociously attacking women of every age and condition" (McNamara, 1996, 33). Religious women were no exception to this consistent historical thread, but they were also treated differently because of the vow of celibacy, which removed from them the greatest objection the Church had (has) to women: their sexuality. St. Jerome voiced this teaching as early as 398 when he wrote and preached that "a woman ceases to be a woman" and may be called a man "when she wishes to serve Christ more than the world" by vowing celibacy (Ranke-Heinemann,

1990, 76). In the following centuries, bishops such as Ambrose, Augustine, John Chrysostom and Basil of Ceasarea—to name only an influential few—(McNamara, 1996) continued Jerome's negation and weakening of women, not the least by emphasizing Mary the Mother of Jesus as a consecrated virgin, thereby raising virginity as the highest ideal to which women could aspire. This belief was further illustrated by the scholastic theologians Albert and Thomas Aquinas in the thirteenth century, who—using Aristotelian biology—declared woman a "misbegotten or defective man" (Ranke-Heinemann, 1990, 185). Aquinas, however, offers the solution for women in his Commentary on I Corinthians (McIerny, 1999): "By taking the vow of virginity or of consecrated widowhood and thus being betrothed to Christ, they are raised to the dignity of men" (334).

Nowhere, however, is the Church's historical attitude towards women more vicious or more starkly seen than in the Inquisition, when—using spiritual means for political and economic gain, and persecuting with torture and death anyone deemed "heretical" (i.e., disagreeing with Roman Church teaching), the Catholic Church of the 15th and 16th centuries led the race for power, both political and spiritual. This period, perhaps the most shameful in a shadowed history, saw the torture, burning and drowning of an estimated 100,000 to 9 million people, mainly women. (Reuther, 1975, 135). In 1486 the Dominican Inquisitors Kramer and Springer (Kramer & Springer, 1973) published the <u>Malleus Maleficarious</u> (<u>The Hammer of Witches</u>) which became the witch hunters' manual "for the next two and a half centuries. Persecutions increased throughout the sixteenth century, reaching their greatest ferocity in the early 17th century" (Starhawk, 1982/1988, 187). In many cases, Church officials seized the land and property of so-called witches, thereby increasing the Church's own wealth and secular power.

This History Today

This is the history that shaped and continues to shape the Vatican Church's view of women: control through imposed authority is its chief characteristic. Yet, despite this ancient ambience of domination and denigration of women in general, Catholic vowed women shine like sparks throughout it, daring the powers and finding ways—even through outer conformity—to bring into action new ways to address the needs of the world around them. Herein lies the distinction, generally unrecognized, between the male clerical-centered, hierarchical Church of the Vatican and the thousands of orders of vowed women. The first is focused on preserving, protecting, and saving the institution at all costs, the latter on serving the disadvantaged of the world. When, however, as several recent writers on the topic point out, that fire of passionate service loses its spark, it is often because the orders and Congregations "become so encrusted and fossilized" in institutionalized structure, i.e. the Church. (O'Murchu, 1991, 47). Religious life "has become domesticated by too close an identification with the law, structure, and spirituality of the institutional Church" (Johnson, 1994, 231).

Even touching the surface of such a history leaves me with the question, "how could all this happen in an institution supposedly devoted to compassion, spiritual values, moral guidance? The old answer – and excuse - of sinful human nature is no longer enough.

The Silence of Catholic Vowed Women

Women's silence about the costs, suffering and isolation of celibacy has muted the significance of their lives to being objects of curiosity. Celibate women have not expressed to each other and others their particular experience of women's ecological struggle with limitation and mortality. (Gray, 1995, 149)

Not unlike their counterparts in Western culture, the voices of Catholic vowed women were not generally heard before the latter part of the previous century. Where a growing feminist influence in North America challenged women to speak out the truth of their own life experience, the same has not happened to any great extent for Roman Catholic nuns, as was demonstrated by the decision of the Leadership Conference of Women Religious—considered the most progressive association of Catholic nuns in North America—to keep private the first scientific study on the sexual abuse of nuns in 1998. (Lawton, 2003.) Feminist influence has provoked some Catholic writers to critique patriarchy and hierarchical structures both in Church and society, (Chittester, 1986, 1995; Fiand, 1990; O'Murchu, 1991, 1999; Schneiders, 1991a, 1991b ; Wittberg, 1991) but it has not reached the realm of personal expression for the large majority of vowed women. It is important to note that the women whose stories are contained in Chapter IV constitute a minority rather than a consistent majority in the Congregations. "Finding one's voice" (Morton, 1985, 20), a basic principle of feminist thought, has not extended to the personal sharing of the life stories of Catholic vowed women, nor of the details of what it is like to simply live this life. Gray (1995) and Rothluebber (1994) make some attempt to speak with the actual words of the women they interviewed, though Rothluebber stated (personal correspondence, 1995) that though "I did write the journal...it is fictional in its details and is a composite of mine and many other women's experiences". Gray, on the other hand, quotes freely from the participants in her study and weaves insights from their words on celibacy, which is the focus of her book. It is interesting to observe that two of the three books I was able to find in the literature that set out to speak from a personal standpoint focus on the effects of vowed celibacy, a topic that is seldom discussed in formal gatherings of those professing the vow, except in theological terms and teachings. Besides Gray and Rothleubber, the third book that reflects more personal experiences of Catholic vowed women was written in 1985 and is an edited collection of reflections (Ware, 1985) of 19 well-known nuns in leadership positions at that time. Each one tells her story in a half dozen pages or so, and each is as personal as it is possible to find; yet, even these reflections are still very much focused on the outer, rather than the inner experience of living religious life. It is also interesting to note that—only as I finish this writing—two prominent writers on the topic of religious life have published books highlighting their personal experience for the first time. Fiand (2002) bases her writing about belonging on the experience of losing her closest friend to cancer; Chittester (2003) her reflections about struggle and the search for hope on very personal struggles with authority that she has had in her lifetime.

Lack of Personal Identity

Because the majority of members of religious communities grew up in a pre-feminist world and entered vowed life usually before the age of twenty, they reflected the cultural norms of their times in that

Like her married sister who delayed developing her personal identity until meeting a man whose identity she could assume, the woman religious forestalled her personal identity search as she learned to accept the identity of her community. (Murphy, 1983, 67)

This lack of personal identity is at the heart of the deep, unconscious personal silence of Catholic vowed women, where an expression of inner experience could begin to tell a different story about our future. Intentional renewal has been the agenda of Congregations of vowed women for the past 40 years, yet that renewal has focused almost entirely on outer change and structural revisions, mistakenly taking for granted the natural individuation of members. A fear of individu*alism*—so different from individu*ation*—has robbed both individuals and communities of the rich diversity of thought and singular gifts needed to retain the vitality of the original founding purposes, appropriate to historical time and place.

The most startling awareness of my own review of writings about Catholic vowed women by far is the realization that—with the exception of the five books cited above, I could find nothing written in the voice of personal experience. Books about religious life are written overwhelmingly in the words of history, theology, sociological analysis, and ecclesiastical prescription. The voices of the women themselves, from a personal viewpoint, are today as shrouded in silence as were our bodies shrouded and veiled not so many years ago. This observation has been confirmed again and again in my encounters with hundreds of religious women over the past 25 years, many of whom cannot give a personal opinion about any topic until they hear what someone in authority is saying about it.

Centuries of Women's Silence

The reason for such personal silence is buried under the weight of centuries, but at its source it can be construed within the parameters of a feminist recognition that our language itself is a male language (Belenky, Clinchy, Goldberger & Tarule, 1986, 203) and that "men move quickly to impose their own conceptual schemes on the experience of women:"

Women have been in darkness for centuries. They don't know themselves. Or only poorly. And when women write, they translate this darkness. Men don't translate. They begin from a theoretical platform that is already in place, already elaborated. The writing of women is really translated from the unknown, like a new way of communicating, rather than an already formed language (Duras, 1975, as cited in Belenky et al., 174).

If this can be written about women in general, how much greater is the burden of such language on religious women, whose lives have been circumscribed by a male hierarchical framework held in place not by academic constriction or governments, but by God himself? By the threat of spiritual wrongdoing, of offending God, even of damnation? Such is the weight that keeps Catholic vowed women in their silence.

For the reality of a male language is not a matter of generic pronouns, but of the dominant hegemony of *a conceptual framework from which the language emerges.* Even women who make every effort to replace male, exclusive pronouns with more inclusive ones still speak in a conceptual framework, still internally configure and prefer language that is structured from that framework. The silence of women could evidence an unspoken—and perhaps an unconscious— choice for the language of women that is as yet unknown. Even those who have begun to speak "from the darkness of private experience" (Belenky et al., 1986, 203) do not have at their disposal a shared public language. The public language in preferred usage expresses a male framework. Feminist insight has removed the walls, but the structure itself needs dismantling now. Morton (1985) writes about this possibility for the silence of women when she credits Sally Gearhart for the phrase "a word we cannot yet speak." Morton herself clarifies the meaning of this phrase when she says:

we agreed that women are having emotions, visions, experiences that no words in the patriarchal language can describe. I want to posit the possibility that there is a word, that there are many words, awaiting woman speech that cannot now be fully described because of a patriarchal language structure. (87)

Morton (1985) reminds us that the silence of women goes much deeper than the choice of pronoun; it goes to the internal structure of the language itself. Changing pronouns from exclusive to inclusive, from the "he" to the "she and he" has not effected structural change. Women still pursue equal pay for equal work (Ehrenreich, 1998), though this fight is more hidden behind the cultural assertion that women now have more choice where once they had none. Further, choice is compromised where original language is compromised, as Morton (1985) and Duras (1975) posit. Goldberger (1996) points out that

it is only those who are silenced by oppressive and demeaning life conditions who feel powerless, mindless and truly without words. The sense of choice about whether to speak or not to speak is missing for such women and men, as is their sense of knowing (346).

Though Goldberger here refers to minority cultures within the United States, I would apply this same description to the plight of Catholic vowed women for two reasons: they are silenced because they are women, and they are silenced by the patriarchal dominance of the Roman Catholic Church. The condition brought about by this silencing can be described, as it is by Mindell below, as "internalized oppression:

When you cannot protect yourself from overt, covert or institutional abuse you unwittingly internalize your attackers, adopt their style, and accept their criticism. You belittle and repress yourself and end up feeling worthless without knowing why. After awhile, you no longer notice the negative thoughts you have about yourself. (1995, 108)

Living and working with Catholic vowed women for most of my lifetime and coming to the place of recognizing my own internalized self-oppressive beliefs makes me sensitive to witnessing this phenomenon. Though motivation cannot be discerned through behavior, and acknowledging that people act from either fear, habit or conscious choice, I notice the women in religious communities who don't leave their bedrooms without a veil, though the rule against doing so has been lifted nearly 30 years, or the ones who cannot depart from institutional prescription no matter how small—like changing the time for dinner, or the ones who consider any questioning of authority an questioning of the Church and any reference to sexuality sinful. These behaviors cause me to wonder whether these women continue to live out the centuries of oppression experienced by women in general and Catholic women in particular. Yet, they are not vastly different from women everywhere who are prisoners of marriages which keep them confined in spirit and sometimes in body, or women trapped in work situations which are structured for men and require women to "prove themselves," or women victimized by social welfare systems that assume they know women's needs without asking women themselves. (United Nations, 2000)

Just as the silence of women in general has not been greatly changed by opening traditional male professions to their presence, so the silence of Catholic vowed women has as yet been barely touched by the so-called "freedoms" resulting from the mandated renewal of Vatican Council II.

The visible changes undergone by nuns since that time are drastic in terms of numbers, properties, ministries, and lifestyles, mainly in terms of external diminishment (Gordon, 2002, 3) During the course of this study, I came to believe that these changes have been clearing the way for the real work, still to be addressed, that is, dismantling the inner belief structures that maintained that oppressive hierarchical authority for so long. Audre Lorde's (1984) classic feminist phrase "for the master's tools will never dismantle the master's house" (37) reminds us that even our language is still a "master's tool." Perhaps this is why, as women, we have not yet succeeded in breaking our deepest silences. The language itself sustains the way we think and speak about what we are only just coming to recognize as abuse. J. Brown and Bohn (1989) offer this reflection: "With every new revelation we confront again the deep and painful secret that sustains us in our oppression: we have been convinced that our suffering is justified" (1). Here is the core of internalized oppression, firmly fixed by a historical containment of "women's place" and sustained by Christian spiritual teaching in which suffering, making sacrifices and carrying one's cross held that internal structure in place. Those walls are still in need of dismantling.

Signs of the Dismantling

And yet there are traces of encounters indicating that the dismantling is happening, mostly quietly, in North America. The stories of the eleven Catholic vowed women told in this book testify to just that undoing. However, even as I am was writing this, another, louder protest is beginning to be heard as reports of the sexual abuse of nuns are coming into the public domain. Like battered and abused wives everywhere, the oppressive environments in which most nuns were formed produced what J. Brown and Bohn call "the false self":

The false self produced by dominance and abuse is a self that rests its self-esteem in winning approval from significant others by empathetic union and/or success

30

and achievement. In either case, the false self is held together by its ability to use others and the external world. The false self has lost the capacity to feel intense passions, and so is haunted by depression. It will idealize its parents and the past, place blame for abuse on victims, and be unable to recognize healthy intimacy. Finally, the false self will seek to reproduce itself in others over whom it has control. (1989, 149)

Cultivation of this false self began in me, and in many other women, I would suggest, in early childhood, but was affirmed and strengthened within the novitiates of religious communities, nourished by a spirituality of suffering and self-denial to a degree that ensured the development of a false self in the sense of J. Brown and Bohn (1989). Highly spiritualized self-negation was considered essential to the traditional vows of poverty, celibacy, and obedience, and opened doors for abuse of all kinds. Revelations of these abuses are only now beginning to be revealed; one of the first public documents to come into mainstream media is a study conducted by the University of St. Louis in 1996 (Crawford, 2003), which found that "forty percent of nuns have been sexual victims of priests, nuns or other religious persons as adults." The St. Louis study is the only national scientific study dealing with the sexual victimization of nuns in the Roman Catholic Church, and it came to light only because of a 2001 statement of the Vatican acknowledging "the problem of sexual abuse of women religious by priests" (Allen, 2001). Reuther (2002) further delineates the situation of priests who not only sexually abuse nuns, but "cruise on their nights off, picking up prostitutes or gay partners in bars...there are also affairs with women...and common-law wives, with whom priests have children." Crawford, (2003) also reported the decision of the Leadership Conference of Women Religious (LCWR) to not publicize the study in the general media in 1998.

A former general secretary of the Canadian Religious Conference which represents 20,000 nuns in Canada, was quoted (Crawford, 2003) as saying, "If someone says 'I have been abused', we do not have a procedure. I swear, we do not talk about it. We would rather die than talk about it" (K2). The St. Louis researchers noted that they believe the figures are more likely underestimated rather than overestimated; the CRC comments bear this out. They also note that "it's not exactly clear how the sexual victimization of nuns compares with the general population; but the abuse results of the nun survey seems in line with many other surveys of women."

The silence of nuns, then, can be attributed – at least in significant part – not only to the primary condition of women-having-no-language of their own, but also to a condition shared with women everywhere: that of overt and covert sexual abuse.

Yet, this is not the whole story either. Just as religious women have been about the work of speaking a more inclusive language but without addressing the underlying structure, so we have been engaged in the work of intentional renewal since the ending of Vatican Council II in 1965, a beginning, at least, of dismantling external walls. This dismantling has included identifiable dress codes, common horariums, scheduled recreation, ministries restricted to Congregation-owned institutions, forms of prayer in common, and assumed understanding of a common language. What appears in the place of all that uniformity is a tattered, diminishing, and divided culture, still using the old language though with multiple meanings. "Community," for example, can now as well mean living singly in an apartment as sharing a house; "prayer" can mean communing with nature as much as meeting in Chapel to recite the Prayer of the Church aloud.

Transformation – not yet

But what is significant here is that, while external identifiers have diminished, inner belief structures remain unquestioned for the most part. As we know now from studies in Transformative Learning, transformation does not happen until deep, internal and unconscious assumptions are challenged and released. Some indications that bear out this observation are these: a consistent refusal by the majority of Catholic vowed women to engage in critical thinking about Church and authority; continued emotional distancing in relationships as appropriate expression of the vow of celibacy (though this might be more habitual than conscious); and an unwillingness to the point of resistance to discuss "taboo" topics such as money, creativity, sexuality, and autonomy. The opening of the Church to the values of the social sciences, specifically suggested in the Council document "Gaudium et Spes: The Church in the Modern World" (Vatican II, 1965b) as a way to develop deeper understanding of the nature of the human person, did not openly support the value of individuation in any active sense, though personal conscience has always been highly respected in Catholic moral theology. However, at that time, awareness of the lesser place of women had not yet begun to emerge.

Like most women, we have yet to be aware that "we cannot learn from men how women develop spiritually. The responsibility for describing this process is ours, as women" (Anderson & Hopkins, 1992).

CHAPTER III:
The End of Renewal

But how do we choose? Listen. We are called into love.
Someone or something appeals to us. We are drawn.
A voice calls us by name.
Our vocation, like our destiny, is not something
to be fabricated, but a response to make.
(Keen, 1983, 115)

Throughout the explorations of this study I came to see and believe that Congregations of Catholic vowed women are at the end of renewal, or we have gone as far as renewal will take us. Signs—such as current recruitment campaigns for new members employing techniques used in the early 80's—indicate a looking backward rather than forward. Who is taking seriously the statistics such as those quoted in Gordon's (2002) article "Women of God": "The median age of nuns in the U.S. is sixty-nine. From a high in 1965, when there were 180,000 nuns in the U.S., the number has fallen to 80,000", or the Canadian figures released by the Canadian Religious Conference of today's median age being 72.54, with a numbers drop from 61,885 in 1965 to 20,879 in 2002? (Canadian Religious Conference, 2002)

What are the footprints of the current demise?

When Vatican Council II ended in 1965, thousands of women left their Congregations. No study has ever been done on this phenomenon; the reasons for it would be pure speculation. In Canada alone, 17,700 members left in the 10 years after the Council (Canadian Religious Conference, 2002). Of those who stayed, many entered with enthusiasm into the renewal process. Though renewal engendered conflict, predictably between older and younger members of the Congregations, engagement with that energy of opening was vibrant and freeing for many. In the nearly 40 years since 1965, I observe at least nine strands of change from pre-Conciliar religious life to the present. Chapters of renewal opened women's communities to a porousness whose recognizable characteristics illustrate this description of the postmodern person according to Endean (1996):

> The postmodern cannot be understood for what it is in itself, but only in terms of what has preceded it: the postmodern is a gamut of reactions to the modern, swinging between two moods: a mood of disillusionment, as previously unquestioned assumptions and standards are found wanting, and a mood of exhilaration, as new and better alternatives are explored, developed and advocated." (93)

Several of the co-researchers interviewed for this inquiry highlight their enthusiasm at the freedoms opened up for religious women after Vatican Council II. They also express their disillusionment at how little positive organizational and spiritual change it has actually effected. But in 1965, following the closed Church structures imposed on women's communities for so long, the mandate "to renew" exploded into a clarion call for freedom. The porousness characterizing a postmodern response (an "anything-goes-for-now" approach), expressed by Seelaus (1999) as the implied belief that "world and self mutually create

36

one another" (61) was a quantum leap for women whose lives had been tightly circumscribed by a teaching that "worldliness" and being "out in the world " approached moving into a state of confessable sin. Yet, remarkably, many women stepped boldly into the chaotic opposite of what they'd been taught and lived.

Nine Threads of Opening to the World

The following nine threads of radical difference from pre-Vatican II religious life begin to lay down the tracks leading to this historical moment—the end of renewal—in which we now find ourselves. These threads summarize not only what I have personally experienced, but what I have observed from a career of facilitating meetings of all kinds for a wide variety of communities of Catholic vowed women.

1. De-emphasizing intellectual achievement.

Prior to the renewal mandated by the Council, attention to individual traits and personal needs were not only *not* fostered, they were forbidden, and this restriction was held in place by a spirituality of sacrifice and humility, practiced in a monthly communal confession of faults. The only openly valued capacity was intellect; nuns generally were, in fact, educated far beyond the general population of women in whatever culture they belonged (McNamara, 1996, 312). Within the congregations and orders, intellectual achievement formed a natural hierarchy in the years before the Council. Lay sisters were part of many groups – these were uneducated women who entered the community for the express purpose of doing the manual labor to support the educated women, mirroring the culture of their time. This class distinction was extremely marked: lay sisters sat at the back of the chapel (those who cooked said their prayers privately in the kitchen.) and in some cases were not permitted to speak to "choir sisters", a benevolent term for those who studied, taught or nursed. In some cases lay sisters were not even permitted to pray the Divine Office with the choir sisters, but were expected to pray it alone.

After Vatican II, renewal activities evolved into a nearly opposite pre-occupation for many orders. Within 10 to 15 years, while many initially pursued programs that updated theology in accordance with the documents issued from Vatican II, a trend towards personal and emotional development as well as body-spirit healing modalities grew quickly to be even more widely pursued. In this milieu, attempts were made to eradicate the class difference between lay and choir sisters, but the divide was too deep, and more lay than choir sisters left the communities, though the numbers of both were staggering.

One effect of this shift has been to diminish the power of intellectual hierarchies in women's communities and to invest major financial support in emotional, spiritual, and physical development. This emergence can be seen as a natural balancing restoration of aspects of the human person formerly repressed in the pre-Vatican II lifestyle of Catholic vowed women. It is also a significant factor in the natural individuation process that has led to the present era of shifting into a deeper, interior transformation.

2. Ecological Awareness and Eco-feminism.

Recognizing the ecological urgency of the planet and placing time and resources into promoting that awareness is one of the ways in which religious women embraced their prophetic role after Vatican II in latter years and not always consciously. The language of ecology began to appear in vision and mission statements nearly 20 years ago, long before this awareness became common in the general population. (See Appendix B). As with many visionary statements, those who write them take a longer time to grow them into reality, and this is the case here. Not only has an ecological reality become increasingly concrete for most groups of Catholic vowed women – moving from basic re-cycling to taking sustainability more seriously - but several groups have committed their significant resources to concretizing their commitment. Renovating buildings, placing land into conservancies, and taking legal means to preserve wild spaces are examples of how women's religious congregations have taken seriously the commitment to the ecological imperative. In 2007, Sarah McFarland Taylor wrote <u>Green Sisters: A Spiritual Ecology</u> , tracking and storytelling the contribution of Catholic nuns to the ecology movement in the U.S. and Canada.

Another window into ecology was feminism. As more nuns interacted in the outer world, they encountered the work of feminists outside the Christian tradition, many of whom linked feminism with ecology: Plant (1989), Spretnak (1991), Griffin (1978), Christ (1995), among others. During the past 5 years, ecofeminist Gebara (1999, 2002), writing from Brazil, bridged a gap between secular and Christian ecofeminism in her writings, which is just beginning to find its way into North American religious life. Though less developed than the ecological commitment, an ecofeminist lens is used by small numbers of vowed women in many congregations.

3. Addiction Rehabilitation, 12-Step and Self-Help Groups.

With rigid structures removed and the loss of many community members, holding together an externally-referented life became impossible for many religious women. Centuries of repressed emotions, denial of intuition, and denigration of imagination took a toll during the last 40 years. Facilities for addiction recovery— initially for alcohol and non-prescription drugs, and lately for recovery from sexual abuse and sexually inappropriate behavior—became familiar names in the lives of many religious women.

Many attend 12-step meetings for different purposes or belong to a variety of self-help support groups. Facilities such as Southdown (Canada) and Emmaus House (New Jersey) are among several rehabilitation facilities offering recovery programs lasting from 6 months to a year for Catholic vowed women from all over the world.

This development "humanized" Catholic vowed women's communities, which are, after all, a microcosm of society-at-large. With such needs being brought into the open, life became more real - if not more difficult - in local houses, and the challenge for organizations to provide for and support its members much deeper than when the life depended on external structures alone. While many religious women have moved through these programs, the aging of communities is lessening present participation, and members continue to live and practice their own healing modalities in collaboration with those of like mind and heart.

4. Strategic Planning and Organizational Studies.

The first two or three Chapters (see Appendix A: Glossary) for most religious communities after Vatican II concerned themselves mainly with change in external identifiers such as habit and ministries. When these had been addressed, some Catholic vowed women began to realize the need for different ways to adjust the structures that these externals had hidden. Even in the 1970s, consultants were employed to help with long-term strategic planning. This signaled an expanding worldview that would have been unthinkable before Vatican II, when the knowledge of the social sciences was not seen as being helpful to spiritual understanding, especially when it was given by "secular" experts.

Since that early consulting, however, leadership personnel of women's communities have used the writings of Wheatley (1996)

Owen (1994) and Baldwin(1998) among others, for the design of congregational meetings, and have been attending workshops and conferences addressing multiple dimensions of renewal efforts, including facilitation, group dynamics and development, They are now moving into the language of transformation, as attested by the last several editions of "Occasional Papers," writings of members of the Leadership Conference of Women Religious.

However, the readiness of many communities to embrace the findings of the social sciences and to allow their groups to be changed by them also throws these communities into conflict with a hierarchical Church not as welcoming to such information. This situation remains despite a clear direction suggested in the Vatican II document "Gaudium et Spes" (1965b), which directly recommends such consultation.

5. Christian Feminism and Biblical Exegesis.

Along with references to ecology (above), so-called "feminist" values began to be mentioned in the 1980s in vision and mission statements of the women's communities (Appendix B). A highlighting of the oppression of women and children stand out in these statements, in startling contrast to the continuing hierarchical male concerns of the Vatican Church.

The opening of biblical studies to Catholics after Vatican II was readily embraced by Catholic vowed women, and some have made biblical scholarship a life work (Gebara, 1999; Johnson, 1994). Using this knowledge, they highlight the role of women in scripture, even in the Old Testament. Many have also become theologians, knocking at the gate of the Church with their brilliant challenges to official Church teaching: (Chittester, 2001; Grammick, 2000, Schneiders, 2000, 2001).

These leaders in thought are pioneers, not only for women's religious communities, but for women everywhere. Their questions, challenges and confrontative statements have opened thinking and action for many women needing inspiration and support for what they are already discerning inside themselves.

6. *Feminist Consciousness and Political Action for Justice and Ecology*

Catholic vowed women have always taken seriously the need for active social justice in the world, using as their basis some of the excellent Vatican documents on justice topics (Walsh & Davies, 1991). This stance, among all the others named, resonates most readily with the original vision of the foundresses. During these years of renewal, many religious women, especially (but not exclusively) in the United Sates, have been arrested and jailed for their justice work, for their protests and for their actions of civil disobedience. From the war protests and civil rights marches of the sixties to present-day protests against the death penalty and the activities of the School for the Americas in Georgia (where military personnel from many countries learn techniques of torture), Catholic vowed women have always been in the forefront of working for justice.

Some Congregations, among them the Sisters of Mercy and the Dominican Sisters, have established "desks" at the U.N. to monitor and influence policy. This recent development demonstrates religious women's increasing realization that poverty and injustice are systemic and political, not about scarcity but about disproportionate distribution.

It was through the doorway of pursuing justice that women's communities became more alert to the plight of women's cultural situation of oppression and deprivation. Some directional statements written as the outcomes of Chapter meetings openly express a special focus on the needs of women and children. In Canada, the recent coming together of several women's communities to raise awareness and protest regarding Human

Trafficking, especially of women and children, is a strong example of justice work with a global vision.

During the last several years, the commitment of women's congregations to Environmental awareness and action has also been escalating. Many participate in Justice, Peace and the Integrity of Creation (JPIC) organizations as well as greening their buildings and protecting their land from developers.

7. Ignatian Spirituality and Spiritual Direction.

Beginning in 1969 in Canada, the Spiritual Exercises of St. Ignatius, more often referred to as "the Long Retreat" or "the Thirty-day Retreat" was opened to women participants by the Jesuit Order of men for the first time in history. Not only did this opportunity encourage the sharing of women's personal prayer experience, but within 5 years, women began to be spiritual directors, a position formerly held only by male priests and one that was considered an automatic given with ordination. Perhaps more than any other experience, this opening for women de-clericalized spiritual direction and invited expression of women's creativity in prayer and ritual. As Spiritual Directors, women came into more of their power. Since the early years after Vatican II, women have increasingly taken on this role in the Catholic tradition, becoming directors of retreat houses and amplifying the Ignatian experience into a broader approach to prayer, meditation and reflective practices of many kinds.

8. Physical, Psychological and Spiritual Development.

Prior to Vatican Council II, members of religious communities were denied any physical or psychological teaching. Simply put: The body and all its functions were sinful. It was, by some communities of both women and men, whipped (literally) into submission every Friday night. In others, a "bathing shift" had to be worn to take a bath, so that one's own body couldn't be seen. Many religious women's breasts were flattened by binding cloths beneath their habits—all this before Vatican Council II. One-to-one friendships were forbidden, deemed sinful, and given the derogatory term "particular friendships," showing a fear of lesbianism in women's communities.

Within a few years, however, not only had these practices all but disappeared, but psychological testing for candidates and programs for personal development of members of all ages opened the possibility for the beginning of individuation. It is no wonder that some could not take that path, given the severity of early training against any sense of self.

Spiritual influences other than Catholic religious practices and Church law began to be sought out as inner spiritual searching led to including beliefs different from those of the Church. While Vatican statements warned against allowing evil to enter through the practice of yoga, some vowed women continued not only to practice it, but to teach and promote it. Some vowed women have become Reiki Masters and massage therapists, Jungian analysts and professional counselors. Longings for earth connections have led others to adopt First Nations ceremony and pre-Christian Celtic ritual as deep expressions of faith , while they might or might not continue to practice Catholic sacramental life.

These developments have led to the current situation described by Schneiders (2000, 213) of vowed women openly declaring their separation from the Roman Catholic Church while remaining members of their Congregations.

9. Process Facilitation and Women Facilitators.

During the last 18 years of renewal another strong but often unnoticed shift has occurred; i.e., that most meetings of all kinds in women's communities, including retreats, are facilitated by women. This would never have occurred before 1965. I can find no reference in the literature to this change, nor what the effects might be.

A large influence in the shift was been a 20-day training course for facilitators designed by Margaret Denis, of Huntsville, Ontario, Canada, called "Process Facilitation." This course, too new to be documented, was designed using intuition as well as reason and imagination, and teaches how to use these human functions along with intellect in facilitating groups. Literally hundreds of members of religious women's communities have been trained as facilitators in this mode, including leadership personnel, on an international scale. My own experience as trained and trainer in this approach leads me to note that Process Facilitation has had at least two effects on Catholic vowed women: it has increased our ability to participate in our own decision-making, whether that be economical, legal or spiritual; and it consistently encourages us to trust and use our own perceptions in the world. A third advantage is that these courses always included women and men who were not religious, and the mix was significant in breaking open the sometimes insular mentality of Catholic vowed women.

Finally, the hegemony of women-leading-women throughout the network of communities around the world indicates such a shift from pre - to - post Vatican II years as to be deeply radical. I also see it as a little noted influence of feminist consciousness rising in our culture (Eisler, 1988, 29).

As Far as Renewal Can Go

These nine threads of visible change, and others as yet unnoticed, have contributed to the disintegration of the form of religious life so crisply defined and recognizable in the world before Vatican II. I also want to concur with Myss, (2001) that the thousands of women who chose to leave religious communities after Vatican Council II have done a singular service in spiritually seeding the world, bringing their spiritual values and devotional practices into a dualistic world of sacred and profane. I am also aware that much more could and needs to be said in each of these areas. Some writers, notably Leddy, (1990) say of this period that we have gone too far into liberalism or into the even bigger sin of individualism, and that it's time to reclaim some of the old ways before the whole enterprise is lost.

I strongly believe, however, that we have not gone far enough, though I do maintain that renewal—understood as deliberate planning for conscious change—has taken us as far as it can. "Renewal," the planned and deliberate action for change, could never be the end of the story because it leaves out the most essential element of real change; i.e., the contemplative, mysterious state of unknowing, of opening to the larger powers whom we cannot know, but to whom we surrender in the darkness of faith and love. Renewal – the smaller-sighted and necessary act of ego and intellect – can only take us to the edge of this faith. We know we are at the end of renewal when everything that used to work, no longer does, when all of our plans fall around us like ashes. Such is the state – I would propose – of religious life now. But this is far from the end of the story. It was really only a stage that allowed us to shake loose of previous thought-holds and life-by-rule. These forty years have taken us to the most dangerous, vibrant, and important of all places: we are standing before the doorstep of transformation.

Recognizing the Doorstep of Transformation

How can we recognize that we are standing before the doorstep of transformation? One of the ways is that we find ourselves looking to the past for answers, for programs, for guides to behavior. We look to what has already worked, even if it was twenty years ago. When we look to the future, on the other hand, we see nothing but darkness, unknowing, no answers, tentative plans. Nothing is certain, many things don't work out.

Our powers have been lost through diminishment and aging, through loss and unexpected death, and especially through the reality of very few women joining, and even less of them in their twenties. The fear that accompanies this kind of seeing is often so intense that it becomes unconscious, and we might find it impossible to stay present to it, losing ourselves in activity, busyness, and trying in all ways to control the outer world in the old ways.

A second way we recognize that we are on the doorstep of transformation is that we are desperate to find answers in the outer world. We find this workshop or that, and we rush off to it. Our planners are so full that friends have to make appointments to see us, and it might be weeks away before they can. This frenzy – and it is very evident in religious congregations now – is the sign that transformation is being resisted rather than engaged.

When we finally step up onto the doorstep of transformation, it is because we recognize the futility of only plans and action. It is because we see that all is not in our hands, even while we continue wishing it were. And it is because we are drawn by an *inner* pull, rather than an *outer* one, towards the Deeper Mystery. The Divine, the Sacred, the Universal Creative Energy calls us away from busyness in the outer world to a kind of vibrant presence, a sitting in the dark, a different kind of action that is paradoxical in nature. For it is only in this letting go of forms that essence can emerge. And that transformation can have its way with us.

Conclusion

When I entered the Novitiate in 1964, one of the first things we were told was that 50 years from now we would be living the same horarium that we were now being taught. The next year, at the ending of Vatican Council II, everything changed within

47

a few months. The feeling of that time was close to what Rich (1984) wrote in her "Love Poem XIII":

The rules break like a thermometer... we're out in a country that has no language no laws...

whatever we do together is pure invention the maps they gave us were out of date by years... (1984, 242)

The spirit of such "invention" is still very much alive in the stories of the women told later in this book. Against the backdrop of oppression, abuse, negation, and invisibility highlighted here, Catholic vowed women continue to engage "pure invention" to change their world in active and concrete ways, sisters not only to one another, but to all women who struggle against conditions and structures that demean their powers. Engaging in this research has shown me that we have needed all these years of renewal, needed the experimentation, tentative explorations and bewildering losses that are still stripping us of energy and form. We need to lose the forms of things in order to find the essential soul of religious life, what O'Murchu (1999) refers to as "liminality," or "the option for the cutting edge" (Dubisch, 1995 in O'Murchu, 1999) that originally fired the founders of religious Congregations. As O'Murchu continues, "the engagement with values, and not the observance of laws, is what the vowed life entails in its primary and pristine meaning." Transformation is the process which brings us into encounter with that pristine meaning.

CHAPTER IV
The Hidden Heart of Catholic Vowed Women
Ten Tellings

LISTEN TO THE WOMEN

for women no longer search for a space
to be heard; they are slowly
creating new spaces.
they no longer plead for the right to speak
they are speaking
(Beijing Women's Conference, 1995)

These are the stories written by the ten women who willingly gave their stories to this study. Though the original transcripts vary from 8 to 12 pages in length, I have distilled each woman's story into 2-3 pages, focusing on how she describes what she means by her "original fire." This edited story was returned to each teller, inviting her further editing as owner of the story. In each case, I also asked, "what are you moved to say now, reading your story?" Finally, at the end of each story, I offer an articulation of how I was affected and changed by these "tellings," a word I prefer to the more commonly used "story," for its fresh and startling aura of drama. You who are reading might also want to notice what happens in you as you read each of these tellings.

I was profoundly moved by the willingness of these women to open up the some of the dark corners of their religious lives. I knew they were doing this because they believed in the desire of this project to bring to words rarely spoken realities about living the life of a vowed religious woman for most of adult life.

Transcribing and reading these stories, I experienced a dramatic range of intense emotions. I was moved from tenderness and tears to a powerful rage, which could be relieved only by fast walking or vigorous exercise. At times during this part of the process I could not speak at all for hours at a time. I knew that what I was reading was my own story, mirrored beyond the differentiating details, calling up from forgotten depths the feelings I could not release at an earlier time in my life.

When all the stories had been transcribed, each woman received the entire package— all the stories—to read through. Many responded with high levels of anxiety once they received their own transcription, expressing worry that they would be recognized, even though initially there was a hesitancy even to use pseudonyms. One woman—Sarah—was so filled with consternation at her speech patterns and how little the transcriber could actually understand, that she asked to rewrite her story, to which I readily agreed. Another woman, Grey Jay, was upset with the transcription, feeling that the speech patterns dishonored her story, and that she wanted to discontinue her part in the project altogether. Several emails and a long telephone conversation relieved her worry to the point that she agreed to continue, though she edited her distilled telling extensively and to her own satisfaction. I felt that her final version was sharper and truer, her point even more succinct and raw than had been originally transcribed.

I interpret these responses as indicators that what the women spoke in the interviews came from deep, inner places from which they had rarely spoken previously and seeing their words in print for the first time was daunting and disturbing for them. Their own words sobered them, in every case, and caused them all to choose pseudonyms, when initially only four chose to do so. I inferred this sobering effect to be a confirmation of my perception that the real life-experience of Catholic vowed women remains mostly hidden, even among those who would say of themselves, "I have made real change and progress in claiming my own experience and sharing it."

Here then, I present the tellings. You are invited to "hear" them, even as you read. Imagine the voice speaking the words, and notice your own response.

Amy's Telling

*(Amy is 50 years old and had lived for religious life
25 years at the time of this telling.)*

My Original Fire ...I know it from the inside out. Often when I'm in a struggle and "up against" something, I know my fire. It compels me to express myself, in voice or image. And it's also about a harmony inside...it has never never left me.

My Mom says that I never turned up in school for the first 2 years. My sisters thought I did, and I would go each morning with them, but when I got there it was so strict I'd just go roaming the streets. Life was—is— just one huge playground, like the one in the park next door to where we lived. This helped me to develop, very early, an incredible relationship with all the world. As I got older, I think this changed only into assuming more responsibility for the playground, because I became a teacher.

I can't really put it into words, but it's something like I know that I'm as much co-creating out there with all others, as God is; with God. I know that I'm part of all that power coming to life. Over the years it's led me to huge undertakings, like antinuclear protests ...but today I'm probably much more aware of the world's woundedness than I was as a child, riding my bike. There's a thing that happens in me that—for example—seeing the leaves come off the trees at this time of year - if I could get and put all the leaves back on the trees I'd be a happy person! They look so barren and bare and somehow wounded, I'm wondering if I could fix them. There's obviously something there around woundedness that I haven't yet come to terms with!

I'm sitting here because I can see out the window. I have to know where my exits are, and where my space is, because that helps me to feel comfortable. I hated the classroom. I hated it. There I had to sit behind a desk where I felt confined and restricted, but out of doors I was in a world that didn't exist in my own family and school.

I don't always know ahead when my Original Fire is going to come out. The earliest I remember—it came out in a drawing that I got a prize for, and my Mom and Dad treasured it. Actually I find that the more I don't need to know the perimeters, or box myself in, or set it up, the more active it is in my creative expression.

Sometimes I wonder why I ended up in religious life. I ended up here because I believed in where Vatican 11 appeared to be moving, leaving us freer. People became so free...I really believed we were moving together to build a better world for everyone. It took me a long time to know that this was not so any longer, and that in fact we are now in a time of severe repression. There are still parts of me that hang on to what could be, because I tasted all that energy and culture. I saw the life in the communities and the parish and the classroom, and I was part of creating it...I still resist fully acknowledging that it is actually over. I do not cope well with hierarchies or authorities; I'll go along until something fully blows up in my face...one of my first awarenesses of that was in my first years as a teaching sister, and at Easter time we weren't allowed to ring bells. They had what you call "Clappers"— two pieces of wood, and it was for the youngest to ring the clapper. Now I was heavily involved in the parish and the school, so I'm over in the high school art room and the Superior wants me to keep an eye on the time and come back and ring these two stupid pieces of wood together to call the sisters to supper.... that's when I know my fire, like it gets to a point of frustration where I think this is absolutely beyond any sense. I really listen inside of me and I know I just can't do that. I'm in the middle of working over there and I couldn't possibly come back and bang a couple of pieces of wood together- it's a bloody obstacle!!! That's my fire, and the following year the "clappers" did not replace the bells!

I went on living my life that way really, questioning things like "why do we have to use Catholic music at Mass?" (I could never understand how you could get your knickers in a knot over the use of music— for me, anything that was going to speak to the students and get them on board, let's do it.) I went on that way until I got elected into leadership, and then I was confronted with all the shit of my first leadership meeting. There was fighting, and I was appalled by the kind of stuff that went on the meeting. I needed some help to pick up the pieces after that. But the key piece for me was when I was appointed novice director and knew I could not carry out that job in the way it had been always done. After my first year as novice director I knew that the religious life I had grown up with I could never actually invite others to live. I knew that clearly. Again after listening really deeply, really interiorly, I knew that I had to make two radical changes to the way the novitiate operated. That's my fire, and it strengthens me to voice and do what I need to.

The vows...yes, I abide by them and they don't mean anything to me in their present articulation in our Constitutions. As they are expressed at the moment, they hold no energy for me. I could equally live this life without them in that they don't call to me with passion and energy. I believe you need to just translate them for yourself in order to live with authenticity. For example, with the vow of poverty, collectively I am not poor so poverty is more about how I live in a spirit of sharing and how I live in mutual relation in everything that I am and do.

It was when I fell in love with a woman for the first time that it opened up parts of me I was unaware were even there. My fire seemed a more pervasive part of me in contrast to a stance of resistance for example. It was freeing and life giving for me. It was about how I could be known. I hope I fall in love again, in the second half of my life.

Amy responded in this way:

> When I read my distilled story, two thoughts came to mind. First, my original fire is strong and very present to me in times of resistance/struggle but much of what I resisted took such a lot of energy for what really didn't warrant it; for example, ringing clappers instead of bells at Easter in the religious community or using non-Catholic or secular music for students in their religious education. There was and is such a divide between religious life culture and the culture we live in that there is a need for transformation in all these areas still. Second, I notice the absence of a deep current of joy in my story, and actually that was the vow I took the day I celebrated life vows along with the formal vows. At this point in my life, I want to rekindle that part of my original fire. So I'm grateful to have read the distilled version because otherwise I may not have noticed its absence so clearly."

I felt jolted by the "crispness" (her own word) with which Amy shows how she survived the oppressive early structures ("clapper" anecdote) and the directness with which she verbalizes feelings about experiences which I hid for a long time, even from myself: "appalled by the kind of stuff that went on at that meeting ;" and "I could equally live this life without them [the vows]." I was especially moved at the ease with which she shared how falling in love with a woman was freeing and life-giving. Most of all, I felt a surge of vitality at Amy's feisty, faithful questioning, which encouraged me to allow mine a clearer voice.

Cora's Telling

Cora is a 53 year old woman, who had lived Catholic vowed life for 32 years at the time of this telling.

My Original Fire is my life source, my passion...the timelessness of being in the space of creative energy. The fire in me is my own voice...nobody else's expectations.

I used to see myself as separate from the universe, it was too big. It was beyond my reckoning, and I felt insignificant in the face of it. Now I see myself in relationship to all the elements of the universe; just as the universe is unfolding and in process, I am part of that process and part of that unfolding. It's an intimate interaction; so what used to be God's business now seems to be more my business, about the earth and the universe and how I'm sustained by it not only physically, but with inspiration and creativity.

The first time I realized this was when I went into the Carlsbad Caverns and actually walked down into the cavernous space in the earth. Like into the womb of the earth. It was so moving I started crying. Instead of just sitting ON the earth, I was being held in the womb of the earth. Normally they don't let you walk out by yourself, but because it was limited season I got a pass and I actually emerged OUT OF the earth. It was a real birthing process and very physically moving.

Reflecting on your questions made me realize how long my fire was underground, and I can remember when I finally became aware of it. Of course I had become a teacher, and then a high school principal, and a good one too—I could make senior boys cry! So one year I asked Maya, a good friend of mine, where I could go for a directed retreat—I'd never made one before. She recommended this Franciscan, so I set it all up and presented myself to her and—of course, you know I want to do everything right—I said to her, "you know, I've never done this before and I don't know how, so tell me what to do because I want to do it right." She said, "put your hands down on your belly and take a deep breath and relax your genitals." And I said, "Holy shit! I'm going to kill Maya!" And she said, "now, when you go for your walk today feel your feet connected to the earth, and when you sit in a chair imagine yourself leaning back against the earth." And she said, "do you have anything to draw with?" and I said, "sure." She said, "draw whatever you want and when you come back tomorrow bring along what you've drawn." So the next day I brought my drawings and she said, "can I see?" and I said, "sure." I opened up the sketchbook and she said, "what wonderful feminine drawings." And I thought what the hell is she talking about, they're rocks and trees. The next morning I got up and I'd brought all this food, and I peeled this big grapefruit and pulled it open and it looked so beautiful to me so I drew it. When I brought it to her she had a big smile on her face and she said, "do you know what you've drawn here?" And when I looked at the sketchbook I realized I had drawn the most anatomically accurate drawing of female genitalia I had ever seen in my life. And she smiled and said, "do you know what it is?" and I said "it's not the grapefruit I thought it was!" And she said, "but do you know what it is?" And I said "woman." And she said, "yeh—go back and see what comes up today." Well, I'd brought a shell along and I did nothing but sit on the floor drawing that shell with an Eversharp pencil for 6 hours. When I got there the next day she said, "did you draw anything?" and I said, "yeh, it was like praying all day." And when I opened my sketchbook she said "Cora, you have drawn the Goddess." And I thought, oh shit, I didn't mean to. And she began to talk about the feminine experience of God, and I was never the same after that day.

The retreat so touched into that creative place in my feminine self that was so deeply connected with God...that I couldn't be a principal any more. In a year and a half after this retreat I'd resigned and was out of school altogether.

I was in a completely different space of truth. It really opened up to me then: That's when I started doing my own work, and that's when I started being more honest about who I was. And it was my voice, you know. I finally knew in the fibers of my being what I was being called to do. And I knew I couldn't do what everybody else wanted, which is what I'd spent a lifetime doing. First, you know— if I was good enough everybody else would love me. In religious life it was— I didn't have a voice—just tell me and I would do it. I tried to figure out what everybody else wanted, and then I would do it. I was very, very good at it. Very, very, good.

But from that day forward, that was the core, that was the fire in me, it was my voice and this was me and it wasn't anybody else's expectations. And I couldn't always stop what would come out, you know. It would just be there, and then only afterwards I would realize what came out.

It came at a cost, though. One of the Sisters I lived with didn't talk to me for a long time, because we had no other sister who could be principal if I resigned. So there was that, and there was also the minimization that comes from society when one takes the road of being an artist or a poet, like—get a real job. It was a painful process to have to name my own truth. It was freeing in the end, but the process of getting there was incredibly painful.

The darkness. I have to go into the darkness. If I get into my public persona for a long period of time, I begin to define myself by my public persona, and that doesn't allow fire to speak truth, it becomes the mask. I know the fire is calling me when I slow down and sit and listen. I can feel it again, I can hear it. If I don't listen I'll reach a point where I just break—into tears, or lose it—I can't think of doing it anymore. I think, Okay, I'm away from the fire, I'm not in my own truth. I have to be faced with my shadow side or some kind of despair; then I see myself.

I know I'm by the fire when I get quieter and slower and grounded and calmer, but at other times I know it when I feel agitated and I can't hold back the truth, I can't shut up, I feel daring and risky, scared but resolved; it's a whole different kind of energy, but both are the fire. It's probably that in-between-bland-performance-self-space that I don't feel the fire.

I remember doing the dragon-fly painting. That's a totem energy for me; I've had to break a lot of illusions in my life. I drew it on a huge piece of paper. I was afraid to paint it, 'cause I didn't know how, and I might mess it up and might make a mistake, blah, blah, blah, the whole litany. And the painting sat under the table for 6 months. One day I pulled it out and I thought the hell with it. I just need to paint it. And so, it was that moment of risk, that daring kind of stuff. And I wet the paper and I started painting it, and all of a sudden it just painted itself. And I'm jumping up and down and I'm laughing and I'm talking to this painting: Thank God I live alone. And I thought, there it is, there it is, it's still there. Because at first my fears and my illusions were that the fire has gone out. But my prayer now is to stay out of the way so that the fire can happen. It's when I try to control and manipulate that the fire is inaccessible to me.

It's that inner fire, my own voice, that has prompted me to act differently from the group norm, like moving to an apartment by myself 8 years ago. And I have to say, as I got more in touch with my creative energy, I couldn't go to church anymore. I couldn't be part of the institution, I just couldn't. I would go to Church and cry, literally cry, because I had touched into this understanding of God that felt so violated in the organized religion of the Church. So I had to make some very tough personal decisions about— you know—not going to Church. I like to think I didn't believe all that stuff, but I was pretty scared something was going to happen to me.

Prior to that retreat (above) I was pretty much the typical "good sister." I did what I was told to do, what everybody expected me to do. That retreat was the major shift. After it, I pretty much knew I had to take my own power. I touched my fire, and after that my life began unfolding in a way that I knew the authority was in me; the integrity of obedience was in me, not outside me. It was opposite to that whole deprivation theology we lived off.

I knew I didn't fit in the hierarchical, patriarchal Church. I describe myself as a pebble in the shoe of the Church. And the walker will either 1) take off his shoe and throw the pebble out, or 2) ignore the pebble. If so, the foot gets sore and possibly infected, and the whole leg will have to be amputated.

My whole search in life is "how do I stay faithful to the integrity of my expression of that intimate self-revelation, God relationship thing so that I can also do the public thing? Both feed the fire.

So I want to be faithful, but I sure want to have a good time doing it!

After reading her own words, Cora responded:

I felt that the experience of being asked the questions and sharing others' stories has invited me back to the cave of creativity. At moments I've felt the flint spark but have yet to get a fire burning. The challenge has been to be faithful to the walk in and to be patient with the slow descent into the intuitive inspiration that lingers more deeply than where I am.

Cora's telling ignited a fire in me that I often feel but hesitate to express directly. I felt strongly connected to her "fire," especially when she describes how the feminine emerged in her drawings without her knowing it, and "only afterwards I would realize what came out". I know the struggle for "honesty" sensing that honesty with herself was first, as it is with me, and that "my own voice" is the fire we speak from. How I resonated with her sentence: "I tried to figure out what everybody else wanted, and then I would just do it—I was very good at it." As was I, until I could no longer choke off or ignore the dissent inside.

Cora helped me to realize that the decision "not to go to Church" in the old absolute way is for me a non-rational one. I sometimes try to explain it as if it were rational, but reading Cora's Telling I became aware that it is a decision made by my body, which churns and nauseates at Liturgies, and it's a decision of my spirit, who chokes and tightens in that environment as if bound and gagged. Which, in that setting, I am. We are. We women are. And there's truth, proclaiming itself.

Eagle Wing's Telling

Eagle Wing is sixty years of age and had been living vowed religious life for forty-one years. A year before this telling, ago, she decided to leave formal religious life, and was dispensed from her vows.

When I have energy, urgency, and when I feel authentic— connected to myself and to God, sort of all together, then I'm living from my Original Fire. Sometimes it's also when I'm misunderstood, or people disagree, or because what matters to them doesn't matter to me. At those times my Original Fire helps me to a place where those things don't matter.

When I was really young, I had a sense of the universe as mystery, and as I grew that whole mystery was attracting me all the time. After a while I called that mystery "God," but it was always myself in awe of something greater and bigger and more than me, and I was always reaching out for it. Later I began to use words like "connection" or "we're all one." Now I feel less of the mystery and more of the connection, so that sometimes I feel the bombing of Afghanistan in the pit of my stomach, and I don't know how I hold all the pains of the world sometimes. Also the joys! And somehow they're all me, and I experience them in my bones, in my guts, in my emotions. And spirituality is connected with all that. It's very central in my life. In the beginning, this wasn't connected to Church. It was experiences of stars or my own thoughts or music or the sea...only later did I think of it in terms of religion, like the Latin or Benediction. The Sacred was there.

So my Original Fire was about wanting to make the world a better place. I felt a certain discontent with the way things were. It was also about responding to this mystery, feeling so connected. The lives of the saints influenced me a lot; they were all my mentors, I suppose. So that kind of heroic life of self-sacrifice was very appealing, a meaningful life in response to mystery. So I entered the community, and doing that with other women was really important to me too.

When I was a lot younger, I was sent on a mission that meant I didn't always do what I wanted to do. But at a certain point in midlife I could basically choose to do what I wanted to do and only that. So I used to say no to doing things that didn't touch me in my place of passion; if it didn't touch that place in me, I said no, I don't have the time.

I made myself unavailable for the Superior-General's job in this way: After being Assistant for two terms, I left before my term ended. Instead I went to India and taught there for a time. Then I completed a D. Min. (Doctor of Ministry degree) and wanted really simple radical sharing with others the life of the gospel. I just didn't want to go back into those dead communities, you know, those blah, bland, and boring communities! I really wanted to do a ministry out of justice and compassion with a special concern for women, which was—after all—the charism of my community. I lived in a small intentional community for 4 years, and it was a good experience, though it caused lots of tension in the larger community.

I was really able to make changes for myself within the community, but the point came at which I realized that they were for myself, and satisfactory to some extent for me, but it wasn't effecting anything different in the larger group. It was the same church, same world, same people...it wasn't radical enough, something like that. And I was always, and am always trying to go back and rekindle the fire...

I remember how excited I was by the Second Vatican Council. I was high as a kite in the '60's about all that ...I mean, Wow ! We could study the scriptures! This opened up so, so much for me. But it always put me on the edge of where other people were. I was always wanting more reform. For example, I was the first to take off the veil, and I'm not forgiven for that yet. I was always in opposition to the norm. I was always losing votes every time we voted in Chapter. I always lost. For years and years I lost.

Inevitably, I became more and more alienated from my community, especially after I became feminist. One of the most difficult differences was my ambivalence about abortion and choice, and coming into a pro choice position. Then, realizing that my church was in another place...I then had to be careful. I'm afraid I wasn't very brave.

Nobody in my community understood the place I was in, not one. After three times attempting to talk about it to somebody, I just gave up. It just distanced me from them, and it distanced me from the Church. I came to realize that there was such a gap between the Church and myself that it was irreconcilable. But the funny thing was that the more alienated I became, the more on fire I was with the truth of going in my own direction. This is amazing to me, but it reached a point where I can no longer practice in this Church. There was—is—a lot of suffering in all of that... alienation for someone who believes in essential connection is pretty traumatic. That's what I experienced: trauma and self-doubt...I think it is a good struggle.

After reading the transcripts, Eagle Wing offered a comprehensive overview of the patterns she found in all of the stories and of the effects of them on her own place:

> I feel our kinship/sisterhood very much and there is something in me about a "Yes—this, is my community, not the one I just left...it seems to be about being on the same journey and knowing how rich and supportive it would be to walk it together. I can't tell you enough how grateful I am to have had this experience.

Eagle Wing verbalizes many of my own experiences: Wanting to make the world a better place, huge excitement about the openings of Vatican II, and being conscious of the "The Mystery" very early. I too am "always going back to rekindle the fire" and coming to her same awareness, that though I am bringing about changes for myself, they are not effecting "anything different in the larger group." Her spirit reminds me that "original fire" cannot be contained for very long in institutional restrictions.

Grace's Telling

Grace is 54 years old and had lived a vowed life for 38 years at the time of this telling.

My real Original Fire is the willingness to follow those moments of feeling expanded, of being held in something bigger where every trace of fear is gone, every trace of fear...it is also present when a question keeps returning, makes me restless...

I used to believe that if I could find the right set of beliefs, or the right feelings or the right way of thinking, and somehow take them on, that would establish my place in the world. As a young sister, I was intense, very devotional, and I see that now as looking for some kind of solidity. If I could just get into this enough, I would feel solid in the world...traces of that have followed me and I catch it everywhere. I think my initial passion in the justice movement was about that. As it happened, I never felt it...I mean, I'd find myself saying something apparently with conviction, and it would ring hollow in my own ears. The same with feminism. I think initially there was the dynamic of now, NOW I have the right way of thinking. And if I can just be strong enough against something else, that will give me my place in the world and my sense of solidity, and probably what I was hoping for was that it would give me a sense of belonging in a group. And again, the real experience of that after awhile was that the words started to ring hollow. I still tried to say them— it was as if I was trying to convince myself as much as anybody else.

There is a strand of this in my present job on the leadership team, though a shift has also taken place. And that's from seeing the world and everything in it as kind of solid, to seeing everything in the world as shifting. It's less about thinking the right thing, and more about what it is I think and feel at this moment. Relationships are in motion—this rings so true for me. And my sense of the universe is that it supports that belief. I look out around me and see everything in motion, and seeing it out there helps me to see it in here too. There's coherence. I feel a part of that constant movement.

I have had a few moments of being taken out of myself, and that's part of what I call my Original Fire. Just moments, but they stay with me. I remember being 18 and walking around the grotto on our Motherhouse grounds and having this very clear physical sensation that I was held by something bigger, and every trace of fear left me. I was carried in that experience for 3 or 4 hours, and then I could feel it leaving, and I started to panic. There was another moment, when I was 19, which lasted only about 3 seconds, and I remember it 30 years later! But the most vivid one around that kind of thing was my first experience of falling in love. I was about 30 and away at summer school—well, if you're going to fall in love you might as well be away at summer school—it was that experience again of being released from fear. It wasn't like walking on clouds at all, it was like walking on the earth, but everything was different. Well, I broke every rule in the book in that relationship, and at some level I knew it was good, in fact very, very good.

Another experience of my Original Fire—the restlessness piece— is when there's a question or a thought returning. And it keeps saying, "you've got to act on this, you've got to pay attention to this. And it's no big thing, but don't dismiss it. There is always something about the lure of another world— you know— beyond the one I was in. And sometimes this "act on it" shows itself in resistance. Asking to go to Latin America was an example of this. I'd been talking a lot about justice issues, but the experience was missing. I'd been teaching 10 years, so to ask for a "year off" wasn't the norm. Still, I went to Latin America, against the norm of the time. Another moment was at a Holy Thursday service in the Cathedral, and when 12 men walked out for the footwashing, I got up and left and didn't even think about it. I was out of there. It was an inner sense that "something is wrong here" and not in a moral way—something askew.

Another way Original Fire works in me is when I want to understand the perspective of another. Once at a Peace March in Ottawa—thirty years ago now—I wanted to go ask someone opposing the protest, "how do you see the world you see?" I notice that in myself a lot, actually. It's not about not wanting to take a stand. It's about knowing that my perspective isn't the only perspective. It all circles back to that sense of motion and flow. There is no one perspective. Perhaps that's the shift.

When I act against a norm of some kind, or an expectation, I feel my own fire, as I did when I was in the election process and spoke fairly honestly my experience with Church. Or when I shared with the leadership team last week that I'm not really committed to the structure of Superior-General and Counselors, even though I'm one of them.

Six or 7 years ago, I wrote a poem that began "I'm beginning to consider the possibility that there's nothing wrong with me."

That for me would be an example of acting against the norm, and applying that to other people too—there's nothing wrong—this is part of that whole flow of peace, of where we all are. It's part of my recurring questions: "Who says who's right?" "Who says that's the only way to think?" "Or who says we have to move in that direction?"

Last year, one of our sisters came to me because she'd inherited $3,000. The usual norm is to hand over such money, as you know, but this particular sister had a problem with money: She never had enough of it! So I said to her, "well, spend the money. Don't hand it in. See what you learn." I'd never tell anybody that I said that! So she spent the $3,000 and just felt what it was like to do that. She came back to me and said, "I've had enough now. I've spent enough now." It's that sense of—we need to find out a lot more for ourselves. We need to see what we think and believe and how we experience to the degree that we'll land at a place that includes us and beyond us. I really believe that. We haven't given ourselves enough room to land anywhere.

I don't particularly think in terms of being a "Catholic vowed woman." I probably think of myself as a woman wanting to live out particular values and caring about this world with other people. I guess that's how I really perceive myself. I keep going back to the belief that we will come up with the norms that make sense if we can free ourselves from the imposed norms, and even the imposed norms on our thinking. We might come back to some of the same stuff, but it will be quite different because we will have chosen for ourselves.

After reading her telling, this is how Grace responded:

I just read my story and felt quite moved by the threads of shifting from static to movement, of trying to see the perspective of another and of giving people - myself included - room, believing that most of the time we come to places that include myself and beyond. I was taken aback by how baldly I told the story about the money. It actually went a little slower in reality. She inherited about $10,000 and I asked if she were going to keep some out, how much would feel like enough— $3,000—then see what you discover.

What actually strikes me at this juncture, however, is the emphasis on the physical— the going to Latin America, and even more, the physical sensation of the experience at the grotto, of physically moving out of the pew on Holy Thursday without thinking much about it. The physical sensation surprisingly has been very integral to key moments. That strikes me because...I am now turning my attention to energy in my body. It has always been there but I probably would not have said that before rereading the story.

For me, Grace's telling mirrors my own growing awareness of my body. My earliest bodily learning was to shut down the pain of physical punishment, and this became a lifelong habit, affirmed by Catholic teaching about the sinfulness of anything to do with the body. For the past years, however, my body has been waking up, and with therapeutic help—I've learned to include body responses in important decisions.

Like Grace, I have also moved from a rigid view of the world to seeing it as a continuous flow of change, and that the restlessness of searching is not anti-spiritual, but an actual expression of spirit "who blows where it wills. We cannot tell where it has come from, nor where it is going" (John 11:21). But what Grace has affirmed for me most of all is that "if we can free ourselves from imposed norms, especially on our thinking, we will come up with the norms that make sense." In this sentence, she summarizes the whole purpose of this exploration.

Grey Jay's Telling

Grey Jay is 65 years old and had been a member of her Community for 44 years at the time of this telling .

I can mark the exact time when I knew there was something afire in me that I could no longer resist, a time when I knew I must choose a different way of being in the world. For many years and many reasons I had resisted the fire, even the acknowledgment of it. Now I have come to know it as the source of my strength and convinced of the energy it gives to truth. I must speak that truth to power regardless of the consequences for myself.

The concept of God is more real and active in my life than ever before. I look back and see myself going around in an unconsciousness that seemed to be programmed into me and sustained with a "wind-up" key. I was caught in a deadness, interpreting the Congregational system as the way to be immersed in life without question. But a moment came when I had the courage and passion to stand alone and say, "I no longer believe in 95% of what I am doing or saying and I am going to change direction.

The moment of decision came about 10 years ago while preparing for a General Chapter. We were being introduced to a new method to determine how the Congregation would be present at Chapter. The idea of self-nomination was being explored, and a year-long discernment process was put in place. Not a bad idea. It was even exciting! As the process began to roll in local communities, it was becoming clear to me that it was all "canned." Real discernment had little place in it. The end result was influenced, almost determined, by the constant flow of literature and directions from Leadership. There was even a suggestion that one could not consider oneself a true member if these directions did not give the desired result. So, my discernment led me to write a statement saying I felt the process was flawed and that I wished to be at the Chapter in my own right as a member in good standing. There was no response to my concern. Total dismissal!

I arrived at the Chapter with my friends on a beautiful sunny morning. Some members of the Leadership team were welcoming people at the door. I was totally ignored as my friends were greeted with great warmth. I knew all was not well and I would soon be tested. At the coffee break, it came. Standing in the midst of a group chatting, I felt a finger in my back. I turned to see the congregational Leader beckon me with a jerk of her head in the direction of the kitchenette. She asked a worker to leave and, white with anger, she said, "What are YOU doing here?" I told her that as a member of this congregation I had a right to be here. She said some things about not obeying the process and then stormed out. I was NOT welcome. Could it be any clearer?

I left, went to a nearby park, and cried uncontrollably. A feeling of isolation, being cut off from people I loved, made me wish (just for a moment) that I had "doused my fire" a year ago and followed the edicts. But almost immediately I was in a rage about these Roman laws that dominate our lives. I saw Chapters as "mandatums" from Rome that are part of the oppressiveness that has kept us bound for centuries. I saw us as a group of women accepting this and affirming this oppressiveness by our own hierarchical system of dominance and inequality.

The feel of the finger in my back and the sting of the "unwelcome" are always with me. But they are an impetus to action, now. I no longer see or feel any negativity around them. It drove me to where I knew I had to go. In fact, I now consider that event to have been my "call" to a higher spirituality. Something inside, like a jet propulsion, sent me over the threshold to where I could live and speak and give passion for truth full reign. I have not looked back.

There was this tremendous grief in that moment. Even now, when I go back to that park I still want to cry. Also, whenever I feel anxious or burdened, the spot in my back where the congregational Leader poked me with her finger starts to ache. It is a "cellular memory" that doesn't go away. I did talk to her several times since then, but she has not changed her view...I did not obey the process she set in place, I had challenged her power and that cannot be.

Over the years I have become stronger in my truth. That's the fire. I often see things differently from the group, and I have the strength to speak even if no one agrees. I struggle with whether I just want to say the different thing just to be different. But quite often I receive solid affirmation from those who want to say the same things but remain silent. They have their own reasons, which I do not want to judge. On the day of the "finger in the back" I became aware of something. I had lost faith in Religious Life as it was being lived. It was clear to me that the old way of the vows as we interpreted them and the measure of control we were forced to live led to a lifeless existence. I would no longer live in that meaningless way. I had to change direction.

I have come to see that dissent is healthy, very necessary to the advancement of truth. Dissent on a global level is keeping the earth from destruction. I add to the collective voice by speaking to injustice and inequality wherever I find it, no matter what the cost. Old structures of male dominance that still bind us and seemingly blind us need to be spoken to...loudly. I am concerned about the number of Sisters who are "unconscious" of these chains. I recently stayed in a house where 12 of the 15 women were walking around dead. I have a heaviness about so much unhappiness among us. Wonderful women...not allowed to live as they need to but as the group (or leadership) needs them to live. I grieve for leadership teams who are merely "maintenance" teams, preserving the "status quo" at all costs. No fire! Original fire is the call of the universe to be involved in life and to answer that call in truth and Joy.

Grey Jay responded to her distilled "Telling" with these words:

It is good. I had a sense of satisfaction in reading it. I want to edit it slightly and will return it to you as soon as possible. Nothing major. You captured the total experience in the distilling.

Grey Jay's telling causes my body to shiver. She states her truths in stark, unadorned language which pierces through my habitual need to modify and soften. Reading her, I know that this need comes not from a concern for the other as much as it is from old fear of punishment and rejection. Grey Jay's words free me from this, however briefly. The phrases of hers especially effecting this sensation are: "Interpreting the Congregational system as the way to be immersed in life without question;" "I no longer believe in ninety five percent of what I'm doing or saying and I am going to change direction;" and " I have come to see that dissent is healthy, very necessary to the advancement of truth."

Kate's Telling

(Kate is fifty-eight years old and had been a member of her Congregation for forty-two years at the time of this telling)

Original Fire is about the visible and the invisible and that my own struggle with being invisible is also at the heart of my original passion. I live in the world trying to make some of the invisible things visible in a way I can only, reluctantly, call "deep democracy."

It's very clear that this essential loneliness is my Original Fire. It's what I have to cry, it's what I do in the world. My story feels like...I am taken care of, I am loved, I am supported, AND I have this loneliness. Which is the cosmic, or the mystery of life, or the dilemma of life on earth. And religious life...I have a sense of loneliness in religious life, and if I left religious life I would have essential loneliness. And if I married I would have essential loneliness. So it's not in any of the forms, but I need to be with some folks that I can connect and around values and vision.

There is something deeply spiritual about what I'm doing, but I don't have words for it. I remember when, just before I made first (temporary) vows, my sisters came down to say, "we know you, we know you, and do you really want to do this?" I was given 20 minutes to talk to them! Twenty minutes—I went to the postulate director and said "I'm having a really important conversation with my sisters and I'd like to stay with them longer and she said "no." I remember standing in the hallway. The Postulate was over here and my sisters were in the parlor over there, and I remember saying to myself that thing from Deuteronomy about life and death: "Choose life. Choose life." And it felt like dead over here and life over there, and why would I give up talking to my sisters for these people over here who aren't talking to me at all?" So I went back and talked to my sisters, and it was a very powerful thing. I remember clearly thinking that with all the ins and outs and ups and downs of my family, it was more a Christian community than this sterile thing we're calling holy. Why could this be holy? This is so formal. And I was aware that my sisters were reorganizing their houses to take care of sick in-laws and we weren't allowed to have an extra person at the table!!!!

So I've spent my adult life in religious life, but I've never bought it. Still, it helped me learn about spirituality and gave me openings to explore different ministries...

Tom [a priest] is also a clear part of my story, and I met him before I made final vows. My friends were leaving [the community] to be married, and I still wanted to make vows AND have Tom in my life, so before I made the final decision I said to the community, "he's going to be in my life for the rest of my life—do you want me to make vows or not? I just want to tell you this because it's not going to be any different—he's going to be here for the rest of my life, I know that." And they did want me to, so I made final vows. But I was aware of what it meant to concretely work it out and stay in religious life, to have to choose to stay when the decision to not stay was quite real.

I think Tom has a very similar essential loneliness that's related to how he knows God. That's where we've always met, but it was more covered over when he was in his public role as a priest. [Tom is now retired.] And as I changed and left the Church—not easily—getting to that point wasn't easy—he respected that. For me it was a way to say, "I don't need to take away what you need to do, but I can't participate in it any more. It's too painful, it's so wrong, I cannot do it. And he...he heard it. I was visible to him. And now here we are—years later—sharing a house! It's two houses, really, but we occupy the same building, and everyone who comes—his family, my family, my community, and the neighbors—everyone who comes says "this is so right." What an amazing thing! Tom was and is such a piece of my life...he made me visible, and once he was my voice in a lot of circles. But then I was my own voice. I came to the place where I was my own voice.

I found my voice when I worked for a United Church parish, and my voice was full of questions. Oh my gosh, why do we think we know the answers? The United Church has almost no symbols and I remember some of the former Catholics in the parish wanting to introduce an Advent wreath. So the people began to say, "Okay," we'll light a candle for the kings, and another candle for the shepherds," and I'm sitting there saying "for heavens sake! That's not what they mean!" And then it hit me: Who gets to name anyone else's symbols? Why do I get to say to these people "this is what this means." Who dares do that for somebody else? Why can't they do it? And then hundreds of things fell away in that moment— God, how could you be so arrogant?

Similar questions happened around my final vows, which I chose to make in that United Church parish and to have the ceremony quiet and private. What I really celebrated was becoming Associate Pastor—then I wanted everyone there! But my final vows—it didn't really touch me. I was at the United Church parish, and what came to me was, "who gets to say what my final vows mean to me?" Someone, somewhere, long ago said," this is what it means," but this is not MY life. I have only one life, and if I'm going to make vows they have to be what I mean by them. And I remember thinking, "Nobody gets to say what these vows mean for someone else...who calls someone else's vocation? Who dares do that for another? Who gets to say what my path has to look like?"

It was in that parish that I also struggled with ordination—it had to do with the robbery of rituals. The rituals got so sterile, so disconnected from human life. I was the first Catholic nun many had ever met. And I'd think, "I'm defining this for these people." No one was there to talk it over so I could say," what do I want this to mean?" So lots of Catholic cultural stuff had to fall away, and I had to figure out what's essential, what's beautifully essential in the sacraments that someone else could understand without being Catholic? God, we've gotten so far away from the essence! Which [the essence] is grounding it all in human life and not so far away from that.

So I looked at Women's Ordination stuff, and I couldn't do it. I couldn't be ordained into this! This is too hostile— it's not here— but I did move into feminist work and it was very important to me, but I didn't want an all-women thing either. It's like, that's not the world. The world isn't just all women.

I was elected Provincial, and I brought all of those questions to that. They elected me without asking zip-all. I was thinking, "you're not even asking me anything important, and you didn't ask me if I even go to Church!" After I got in I realized—we've been using feminist language, but the structures aren't feminist. Becoming Provincial with all my feminist background put me squarely into the patriarchal stuff. And I realized, "I'm a public person in this patriarchal stuff right now. O my God, it was easier to be a feminist NOT in a public role. It's public enough to be a nun!"

At the end of a turbulent 6 years they were voting for the new administration, and the conversation is "O my God, what if we elect someone who doesn't go to Church"—by then it had become more common. So I said, "Well, it already happened. It's over."

So I don't have a lot of energy left now for creating something. And I don't want to be in public places as a public person related to religion. I don't want to witness weddings or give homilies. I don't want to do any of the forms that we have left over to express it. I'm trying...I'm still trying to express this thing... something else I have to make visible. Something wordless. It frustrates me, something about...for the earth and so many in conflict. I don't know. I don't know.

I knew that essential loneliness in childhood...feels like it was born in me or something. I would always search out contemplative space. Out of all my experience has come more questions, like "who's to say what someone else's vocation is? Who can dare say who's in and who's out?" Religious life is a massive mystery, and how it achieved anything and held together is pretty fragile...this is such an amazing thing that only mystery holds together.

Kate responded to her telling:

Thank you so much for the distillation of my story. That is a strange experience. I found it old in some ways and new in other ways. The stories were so familiar but the lifting out the pieces to shed light on original fire was powerful.

I most resonate with Kate in her questions and in her sentence, "I came to the place where I was my own voice... and it was full of questions." Here are the ones from Kate that repeat themselves in me:

Why do we think we know the answers?

Who gets to name anyone else's symbols?

Why do I get to say, "this is what this means?"

Who calls someone else's vocation ...to say what my final vows mean to me?

Who dares to say who's in and who is out?

Kate further resounds a conviction of my own when she says, "so lots of Catholic cultural stuff had to fall away, and I had to figure out what's essential. " There is also a loud echo for me in how Kate sees herself now, following a pull towards "something wordless I have to make visible."

Margaret's Telling

Margaret is fifty-seven years old and had been a member of her community for thirty-six years at the time of this telling

My Original Fire has to do with desire and attraction. It's a sense of urgency, aliveness: It's God. It's not exactly courage, because it's such a strong drive... sometimes I would call it an earthquake of spirit.

I grew up in a world that was peopled with saints and angels, and one of my favorites was the souls in purgatory, with whom I had relationships, because if I prayed for those abandoned souls they'd owe me! Also, I'd often talk with my guardian angel, and the saints were advocates, and God was a bit remote and distant. They were all there...people who did brave things, and the spirit of them all is still alive for me. Now it's more that creation speaks with a thousand voices, and God has a thousand faces. That's the shift from then until now.

But the most profound shift in my world was getting sober. It was a real hitting bottom for me and at that point I felt I had really destroyed everything and everyone that was of any value... I was in jail. Nuns go to jail for social justice causes or as part of the peace movement. Most of them don't wind up in the drunk tank, which is where I was. Actually, I wound up there twice, but the first one I didn't remember. The second one, I do remember. I felt so empty, and I had nothing left, of course, nor anyone. And it was just a little spark, not much, it was just enough, phew, to make me think I could get well. My Dad had been an alcoholic and died of alcoholism, and I was full of myths about what that meant. What was unique about my second time in jail was this sort of sense, this little sense, that perhaps I could do it, perhaps I could get well. It was an upheaval. I had to examine and reconstruct really everything in my life. In my first year of sobriety I was just going it alone in the room. Oh, I knew about conversion, and I talked to other people about conversion, but I never knew it was this deep, this hard, and this encompassing. Like this, pulling my life apart, and yet I wanted it to happen. I remember thinking, it's going to happen...just show me, just show me, and I'll climb up there on my hands and knees, I'll do whatever I have to do to reconstruct my life.

I always had a deep longing for connection. As a child, I loved having pen pals. It was so exciting to send a letter out into the world and get one back! I would even write to the Rogers Corn Syrup Company and fill out coupons and get all this free stuff in the mail; it made me feel connected, like I was someone in the world. And as kids we were always forming clubs, which never lasted, but it was fun creating them. My original fire was in all that, all that longing for connection.

As an adult, I sometimes feel my Original Fire as an earthquake of spirit. That's what happens when I am exploring my sexual identity, my sexual orientation, my sexual being, which is still uncomfortable for me. I'm so struck by how like an earthquake all that is: Earthquakes often heave up land that wasn't there before, subterranean land, below the earth shell. It was like that for me when I began to look at my sexual questions. One of our sisters asked could she speak to me, and when she came, it was about thinking that she might be lesbian, kind of looking at that. And when we were sitting on the couch talking about this, I remember thinking, "why are you asking me?" And in that moment I thank God I had the grace to say to her, "I want to speak with you about this not as someone outside of it but as someone who's looking at it herself." The next morning I woke up saying, "Oh my God, did I ever say that?" I've opened my mouth and there's no going back. So that's what I mean: It was my Original Fire that makes me know I have to do something, whether I want to or not, and I did want to. Another time that comes to me is standing on the edge of Lake Manitoba in springtime. When the ice is cracking, it makes hollow cracking noises. I was just at the end of my drinking career, and I felt the words coming to me: I said to the lake, "your frozen days are numbered." In retrospect, I know I was saying this to myself.

I know that a part of what interested me about religious life was to be about something larger than my own life. I made vows in 1974; we could write our own vows—within the Church's guidelines—but that allowed me to shape them with a kind of personal meaning that allowed me to live with some kind of integrity. Because if I had to live within the institutional Church as a religious, I would go crazy. I mean—it's just over there, doing what it does, and often it's tragic what it does and, to my mind, needs to be resisted. But I have to live in another, larger kind of church, like a community... the Church that I live in is the People of God. And recently I've begun to think more that the Vatican has left the Church; a lot of religious leaders have left the Church. The people are still there. The Vatican closes off the pulse of life, the pulse of people. I know I don't want to belong in that way. We have discussions about the vows in my community, but they're very predictable. They don't touch reality.

When I take a stand like that, its like a fire burning inside, it's "that's what I have to do." Something has to come out or I'm going to burst. I have to find a way to sit so that I don't spatter all over the place, so that what I have to say gets focused. Another thing I realized while doing this is that I often only recognize I've changed when I've walked quite a distance down a road and then looked back and realized the steps that took me in a different direction.

When I feel alive, when I feel energized, then I know that I'm very close to my truth, and when I'm close to that place there's an energy and lightness in being that carries me.

Margaret sent this response to her telling:

In 1983, I was one year sober and studying in Rome. I went to the English AA meetings, and there met a man who was a religious, on the General Leadership of one of the men's orders. I have forgotten his name (though I think it was Tom) and his order, but I remember very clearly some parts of the conversations we had.

One of them was when we were talking about the blessings and struggles of sobriety, and he suggested to me that he and I were indeed blessed, and that we could write our "Magnificat" every morning. I took that to mean living in gratitude—and have sought to practice that ever since. I also, later that year, put pen to paper and wrote a magnificat for myself.

When I read through the accounts of all the research participants, and particularly my own, it came to me again, that the only response was gratitude—and that I wanted to return to the Magnificat. So I did. So much of what I wrote was still appropriate almost 20 years later, and I have added to it in terms of where I now see myself.

So this is probably much longer than you ever wanted—and much longer than I ever thought it would be—but I send it to you as part of my grateful response to reading my story. It's been quite a trip, and I am so grateful to God, to my inmost self, and to the other persons who have walked with me for long or short times through it all.

Margaret's Magnificat

MY SOUL PROCLAIMS THE GREATNESS OF THE LORD

> **From within my small body, within my small world, my soul bursts forth.**
> **Out of the immensity of inner space, into the immensity of outer space,**
> **I shout your greatness, your heart-wrenching goodness.**

AND MY SPIRIT EXULTS IN GOD MY SAVIOR

> **You disclose, moment by moment, the truth I am learning:**
> **Out of desperate Brooke's and profound helplessness, your eyes were drawn to me, your arm gave strength to my fragility, your life breathed newness into my death.**
> **Day by day, you give strength to my shadow self.**

You transform this place of unique suffering into a place of light and integrity and love.

BECAUSE GOD HAS BEEN MINDFUL OF MY HUMBLE STATE

Afraid you had forgotten me, I wandered recklessly, until broken in the exhaustion of my own resources, I discovered myself, just barely breathing, as your precious daughter.
I caught your glance, so tender, so longed for, and within me stirred the ache of tears and a long forgotten joy.

YES, FROM THIS DAY FORWARD ALL GENERATIONS WILL CALL ME BLESSED.

Such an extravagant boast.
And yet in a small inner corner, I know it's true.
Your transforming goodness is not for my lifetime only,
but in some mysterious way, impacts upon the cosmos.
From (that lifetime) of brutal tearing apart and gentle mending, to 'this day', new each morning,
You reveal yourself to me, and to all generations as a tailor of the heart.

FOR THE ALMIGHTY HAS DONE GREAT THINGS FOR ME

It is you, God of tenderness and compassion who have done in me what I could not do for myself.
Even more generous, you have imagined in me, what I could not imagine for myself.

For your many wonders, great and small, I thank you.

And most of all, I thank you for giving me back to myself, as your first gift to me as the temple where you dwell.

HOLY IS HER NAME

Drawing me, luring me, seducing me, into the silence, into the holy dark, into the original fire.

HIS MERCY REACHES FROM AGE TO AGE FOR THOSE WHO FEAR HIM

In my life, in all lives—as it was in the beginning— Your mercy over-arching all the stumbling, all the groping, all the messiness and chaos.

SHE HAS SHOWN THE POWER OF HER ARM

In ways so variant from how I anticipate.
When I look to the north
Your power disarms me from the south.
When I plead for thunder and lightning,
You come with a gentle breeze.
When I cry out for security, you reveal to me the wisdom of insecurity.

HE HAS ROUTED THE PROUD OF HEART

Beginning with my own, and what a rout it's been, what a rout it is.

But I have caught a glimpse of your face in these moments, that I find so attractive, and that I want to follow.

When the millions of stars that I imagine for myself
lie fallen and broken, in my arms and in my heart, in
those moments, through my tears,
You disclose the bright morning star and the dawn of
a new day.

SHE HAS PULLED DOWN PRINCES FROM THEIR THRONES AND EXALTED THE LOWLY.

There is still a strong part in me that feels that princes
and princesses have all the best breaks, all the best
lines. Princes and princesses seem so assured,
so much in control. I allow their presence to lecture
me to perfection. Perfection
without weakness, without fear, without error,
without confusion.
And yet you remind me again and again to live in
the truth of me – lowly, fragile, splendid, in need of
a saviour.
You take me in your arms and breathe over my broken
life and broken world
the words I long to hear – "This is my body".

THE HUNGRY HE HAS FILLED WITH GOOD THINGS AND THE RICH SENT AWAY EMPTY

I dwell within this mystery and feel as if an inner
knife is scraping my eyes clean; scraping my heart
free.
I know hunger, and I know thirst. I know the illusion
of being rich.
And I know the freedom that comes as you strip each
of my certainties away.

SHE HAS COME TO THE HELP OF ISRAEL HER CHOSEN, MINDFUL OF HER MERCY.

You come, not in a distant way, but in flesh and blood,
in sweat and tears, in joy and tenderness.
You come in other persons, bonding our hearts together
as we suffer, as we cry, as we bow under the weight of
our incapacity and poverty.
You come in warmth and light and wonder as we touch
upon the mystery of one another.
In all these moments, you move between us so tenderly,
stirring up the fire of hope, revealing all the love you
have poured into our hearts, all the courage, compassion
and delight – drawing us to a fathomless joy, to a hint
of the infinite, to a moment where we know you and one
another by that evocative, beautiful name: FRIEND.

ACCORDING TO THE PROMISE HE MADE TO OUR ANCESTORS

So I hold on to the promise, and to you, God of the
promises.
You do not fail us nor forsake us, never abandon us.
Your promise is true, and it softens the starkness of
waiting, by transforming it into moments of joyful
hope.

OF HER MERCY TO SARAH, ABRAHAM AND TO THEIR DESCENDENTS FOREVER

I stand in a long tradition of persons who have waited
for you, groped for you, run from you, wrestled with
you, been overpowered by you.

What they came to understand, I discover over and over again - your mercy.
Your mercy which is over all your works,
Your mercy which suffers with us, undergoes with us,
companions us each step of the way.
Your mercy which grabs me by the scruff of the heart and impels me to be merciful.
Your mercy that moves with such delicacy and reveals to me the secrets of my own heart.
Your mercy that gives vitality to my days and peace to my nights.
Your mercy that sustains my original fire.
Your mercy, my God, fresh each morning, calling me to live.
Your mercy which gives friends to love me.
Your mercy that enables me to love.
For these, and all your gifts, I sing with all my being:
"MY SOUL PROCLAIMS THE GREATNESS OF THE LORD."

Rome, June, 1983
Toronto, December, 2002

When I read Margaret's story, I recognize within myself that my deepest longing is for connection. This was always the case, but only in the process of writing this dissertation has it become undeniable. Up to recently, it is something I didn't want to know about myself. Margaret's description of original fire's presence is also close to my own: it "makes me know I have to do something, whether I want to or not." Seeing this to be true reminds me of how often I'd rather not know what I'm knowing, or say what I'm seeing. More often than not.

Mary's Telling

Mary is 74 years old and had been a member of her community for 52 years at the time of her telling

I can see that my Original Fire has always been about moving beyond what was. For me it's about letting go of fear, and moving beyond the perception that somebody else mightn't like who I am...

When I was young, the world was very small, and it was the same in early religious life. In fact, the world of early religious life was even smaller, because the training was so limited and restrictive. Mostly what I could see was the corridors and walls and the darkness in everything. Even my earliest life in the small town was brighter and had more life in it than that!

Today I see the world as quite expansive, including not just our little planet earth but everything in creation. I experience the whole of the universe as one great act of creation, one ongoing liturgy, and I often think of that when I go to the narrow confines of our own liturgy and our own Church, which is just a little microcosm.

I feel that I first began to experience my fire when I was a child, and it came from part of our daily awareness for including people who had less than we had. We grew up sharing that way— if we had a little ham for Sunday breakfast, for example—every other day of the week it was porridge—one of us would be sent to some other house in the harbor with some of the ham. And Sunday afternoons we would go and visit people who were sick and elderly, even if all we had to bring them was to sing a song. It was a little happiness for them.

There was a kind of freedom in that, but over the years my night dreams have been filled with institutions—like big Motherhouses—I think they symbolize the formidableness of it all. I was forever—not as much now—running and beating up against the walls in those dark buildings and corridors. Sometimes I do get out, and then I'm always running free in open fields. But I also know that I'm embedded in the other, the old life of the walls and corridors. There's still a fair bit of that around me, and there's a tension there almost all the time.

The earliest I can recall my Original Fire is the sense of freedom I'd get from being sent outside my home to do something for someone else. I remember once that my uncle was sick and there was someone up in another cove with a certain bark from a tree that would help him. So one morning I got up bright and early and went all the way to his house and got that bark and brought it to my uncle so that we could steep it out for tea for his illness. I remember the sun on the snow as I skipped out over the hills, and there is such a sense of freedom and purpose in this memory. But I'd have to say I really felt my fire when I left home and began teaching at a very young age and fell in love... there's a theme in my life of needing to be outside whatever structure I'm in, needing to get away from it.

Then I really felt my fire when I was Novice Director and could really teach and make things different for the young women. We were so passionate about the freedom given by Vatican II, we were all on fire with it. But the contrast between the passion and the reality was so great... it's still like one big missing piece. I don't think much really happened, and I feel a great loss, a great loss. Being part of all that sort of isolated me from the old structure, but if I wanted to survive, I had to stay back in that structure. It continues to be a struggle. I'm in tension between two worlds, even now. What I want to do and what I have to do are always in tension, so it's like I'm in that first phase of surviving, all the time.

But I also have moments, like at one of our Chapters, when I said yes to doing a liturgical movement for prayer. Usually I'd say, "oh no, I can't do that, I don't know how to do that," or "I'm afraid to do that." But this time, it was like I was casting all the fear aside and it was symbolic of letting go of everything...just going through the ranks... I didn't plan to, but

I found myself just zig-zagging in and out. It was a moment of letting go of a lot of fear and the trepidation I put around myself, more often than not. When I can manage to go with a moment like that, it's like the fire goes out of control, and I'm left with deep gratitude for those moments. I'm less intimidated by either myself or the group. Whereas if I feel the impulse to do something spontaneous like that and don't, I'm more afraid. The fear blocks everything in me. Then I just keep putting more emphasis on being afraid of doing something rather than letting the fire burn and spread out.

I have broken away from a lot of structures in my life, now that I'm thinking about it: expectations of leadership people after I'd finished my own terms in leadership, expectations of the leader of a teaching group I was involved with, and not just professional expectations he had, but personal ones. That was a big one—I broke with a lot of friends in getting away from that group. There's a cost to all this, of course. It's the cost of silence. Nobody speaking, nobody making a response to you when you know you're right, or mumbling after I've left the room. I can hear it, after I've said something "unacceptable." In one situation, I now wait until others have spoken, because they often wait to see what I'll say before they speak.

It's a long time since I actually thought of myself as being a vowed religious woman. I don't have a lot of excitement in me about being in a Congregation, you know. I'm OK, but I feel that a lot of the things we worry about are still holding on to structures and holding on to a patriarchal approach no matter what we say in Chapters. The vows don't mean what I used to think, or what I taught either; they have evolved in how I understand and live them.

I just feel comfortable with who I am right now. I don't make great big breakthroughs, but I do make them in gentle and subtle ways. I still try to respect and integrate what is needed to sustain ourselves in the structures that we're in. I feel like a circle, and in that circle is a little bit of all of me. I feel myself making little footprints in all these byways and inroads, and I make new little paths, and I feel strong.

Several weeks afterwards, Mary responded to her story in this way:

This process has awakened me to see the panorama of my own life and to bring into focus what I now see as the blessings of the choices and the non choices in the commitment I made a long time ago...the blessings of the joys and the struggles had been lost or buried until my life was awakened again by your invitation to journey with you.

I am aware of the ways in which I have grown and continue to do so, making choices to work with what helps me integrate my mind, body, and spirit, and I am grateful to have lived beyond the structures long enough to know that the richness and the goodness of God lies in that movement towards freedom.

As the oldest of the co-researchers, Mary's story moves me differently than the others. I recognize in my life a similar thread as hers in her words, "there's a theme in my life of needing to be outside whatever structure I'm in, needing to get away from it." I shudder in the same ways she does within the walls of institutions. I consider it an astounding testament to her inward strength and capacity to stay connected to her own passionate energy longer than any of the rest of us. Her story stirs my own hope that life can be so triumphant within an almost prison-like structure. Her words give light to my own path and also make me smile with a surprising joy.

Sarah's Telling

Sarah is 54 years old. While participating in this inquiry, she requested and received ex claustration (see Glossary) from her Congregation, of which she has been a member for 36 years. She has since been dispensed from her vows.

I know I am acting from my Original Fire when I feel whole, alive, and energized ...also when I feel discomfort and restlessness. I may not know the next step, but I know there is an urgency to move or change.

When I was a child growing up in a small town, there was a sense of the abundance and providence of nature. But as a young adult, I saw the world according to the Genesis creation story wherein man was supposed to dominate and subdue the earth. Then, as a young sister, I was often conflicted by the biblical injunction to be in the world but not of the world...somehow the world was evil. Later in my adult life I was introduced to patriarchy and ecofeminism at Toronto School of Theology and it was there that I experienced a major shift in my understanding of the earth. The world changed for me significantly from then on.

An important part of that change was seeing my sexuality as gift, whereas my formation in the Catholic church and my Catholic family caused me to regard my body as bad. During my study of ecofeminisn I discovered a feeling bond to the Earth Mother that really nurtured me as I had not felt a deep connection to my own mother.

Now I feel that waxing of the moon and the energy of the ocean. In down times I feel connected to nature and to the energy of so many women who have helped me in my many rebirths. Now it's picking berries in the late summer and fall- the blueberries, the partridgeberries—that's the fall ritual that reminds me of the extravagance and voluptuousness of the earth.

But what I would now call my "Original Fire" really happened long before that, and in two ways. In my high school years, I often went with my mother to deliver clothing to a very poor family in my community. The children were naked, covered in scabs, and sleeping in compounds similar to the ones used to store vegetables. The mother was helpless, wearing a nylon dress and tearing boards off the walls to burn in the stove. My mother did an intervention with social services to help that family. After that, I felt an urgency to help people in similar circumstances, and I still do.

The second way I'd say I felt "Original Fire" then was in my last year of high school when I had an interior, very personal experience at Mass of being loved by Jesus who gave his life for me. I FELT that love. It was pretty profound, and I felt that an appropriate way to respond to such great love would be to become a Sister, because you know the sisters taught me. Joining the community really covered the two experiences: feeling that intense inner connection with Jesus and the urgency to help people less fortunate.

I've already said how I know I'm being called to move or change when I feel discomfort or restless. This has been happening for awhile now in controlling, institutional communities—they de-energize me and compel me to seek more spacious, life-giving groups. Also, the patriarchal Church disturbs me and does not stoke the embers of my fire, so I have to move away from it as a place of ministry and a community of worship.

Leaving the parish where I was pastor for 6 years caused me deep grief because I loved the work and the people and the opportunities to create and nurture faith communities. Every weekend for 6 years I rewrote the prayers and the psalms in inclusive language for the people. But the hierarchical demands became life-draining, and to be true to myself I had to resign from parish work.

So my Original Fire often places me in conflict with others' expectations. Even very early...like when a person in authority wanted me to go to summer school in Canada because it was cheaper, but I chose to go to the U.S. because of the courses and the emphasis on community. Also when I was younger, the superior wanted me to teach music; I tried it but knew in my soul it wasn't my gift, so I had to say NO, I cannot do this any more. And I was asked to go as principal in an isolated area, and I had to refuse.

A new way I am experiencing my Original Fire is by being present with the disadvantaged women with whom I now work in a kind of "in-the-moment" way, a go-with-the-flow presence of just knowing in my gut what to do. I am moving towards being more flexible and relaxed in this...it's even a way in which I'm breaking away from my own form of activity and busyness.

I have felt my life to be one of community and service and hardly ever looked at myself as a vowed woman, even though I publicly proclaimed them in 1975. I always felt that on some level I could not defend them. On a daily basis I am unconscious of them except when I struggle with authority, with the poverty of the economically poor and with my own sexuality. And in those struggles, reflecting on the vows has not helped me. When I reconnect with my Original Fire of responding to Jesus' love and helping the poor, I do not feel that being a vowed woman enhanced those experiences at all. But my life in community did. That sounds confusing, but it's what I've lived.

Telling my story this way feels like a cleansing and a reclaiming of power and fire.

Sarah responded after reading her story:

In bold print italicized opening sentence speaking of Original Fire I have written *'I may not know the next step but I know there is an urgency to move or change.'* So it is that I have been led to take a period of ex claustration from my congregation. This decision came from my core in January 2002 because I had been feeling a sense of disconnect with the life and direction of my community. Since then I have turned down a job that last year I would gratefully have taken because I would have thought it was in sync with my spirit. One hundred and twenty hours of transformational cellular healing and reflecting on the stories of the women in this process led me to deep knowing that the shadow side of joining the community was strong and externally referenced. I am in process of discovering my true spirit. And discovering my new path is a break away from the activity and busyness of the first half of my life."

I stand with Sarah in the deep midlife struggle for soul integrity; that is, staying faithful to one's own path, which so often—especially in the close knit culture of a religious Congregation— places us in conflict with the expectations of not only authority, but of co-members as well. I hear her echoing my life experience when she writes, "on a daily basis I am unconscious of them [the vows] except when I struggle with authority, with poverty of the economically poor, and with my own sexuality. And in those struggles, reflecting on the vows has not helped me."

Terra's Telling

Terra is 60 years old and was a member of her community for 34 of those years. In 1994, Terra received dispensation from her vows

My Original Fire happens when something grabs my mind and heart so clearly that I pick up and move to wherever I think it's going to happen...

I used to believe that we belonged to a static universe. It was formed and you fit into it—I guess that's why we were always looking to see what God's will was. But now, with an expanded universe that is unfolding every moment, it's not about looking for God's will so much as looking for opportunities to be in the flow. And so the whole journey is one great flashing show...

I guess the woundedness of people was the focus of my early years, and that transformed into the woundedness of the whole planet. The first time I remember being aware of this was when I was a Brownie (pre-Girl Guide). Our Brownie Leader took us to see a group of Brownies who were handicapped. They were quite severely handicapped in ways that I can't...my only memory is of being there and knowing that strange and horrible things had happened to these children, and yet here they were, Brownies like me. I had a feeling that I'd like to know them, be with them. So when I was in Grade 8 I remember telling my teacher that—yes I wanted to be a teacher—but I wanted to teach special kids. It's a bit of a surprise to me that compassion is at the root of it.

But it was this compassion that led me to L'Arche, and it was there that I went against "expectations," and I believe it was my own fire that brought this about. We had a Jewish young man and a Baptist young woman, and it bugged me that they were marched to communion every time there was Mass. What were we doing? Once the director was away, and one of the women had a friend who was an Anglican priest who was coming for a visit, and she wanted him to say Mass. Which he could; he was familiar with everything. So I thought, "we make everyone go to the Catholic one; why can't we make everyone go to the Anglican one?" So I invited the seminarian next door, and he was outraged that I would go to communion at this event and that the event took place at all! And that was in 1972, and I was chastised by the Diocese for it! Now I choose not to go to communion at all when I do go to Mass. I just go for funerals or weddings or invitational things, you know.

Then there was when I first came to realize the whole feminist thing. I went with another sister to pick up some photos at the Mall. When she came out we just sat in the car to look at the pictures, and this guy banged into the back of our car. So we got out and called the police. When the policeman came, he would have nothing to do with me. He wouldn't talk to me, he wouldn't even look at me; he would only deal with this guy. We thought it was quite obvious what had happened, so I was quite shocked that the guy was saying we'd backed into him! I was saying, "no, no, that's not what happened. I've got a witness here." And the policeman said, "oh yeah, sure. Sure, that's your witness." So he just turned to this guy for all the information. Then he turned to me—he'd let the guy go. When I gave him my ownership he saw I was a Sister and he totally, totally turned around! He began to ask after one of the old Sisters who taught him, and on and on. But for me it was a double whammy—what it was like to be treated JUST as a woman and what it was like to be treated as a religious woman, and after that I was asking, "what's this all about?"

I also remember being with a Congregational Leader of a group who couldn't get their Constitutions approved by Rome. I said to her, "well, why do you need them approved? Just go on living." And she said "well, then they'll take all our assets." And that was when I realized, "Oh my God, we're really kept women." We didn't have our protest any more. That was very hard, very hard, and a very significant time for me.

This and similar experiences led to the clarity I felt about leaving the community 6 years ago. But I still struggle pretty constantly with "how am I free, and yet how am I so dependant on structures?" The fire led me into the whole ecology movement, and that's at the heart of who I am, yet since I left the community I am still searching for a new tribe, a new place to put the fire.

It's as if my access to the fire is blocked in some way. And I notice how uncomfortable it is for me to be at the center of the story at all, to really look compassionately at myself.

Terra did not respond to her distilled telling for a long time. Three months later she told me that relating her story had plunged her into such profound angst that she knew she had to deal with yet another layer of the sexual abuse she thought had healed. Reading her story back, she had the impression that she was trying to make a life appear that wasn't really there. Further, she could not even talk about that until very recently.

"Unfolding every moment ...and looking for opportunities to be in the flow." Terra's description of where she is in her life now pinpoints the deepest desire of my own spiritual practice. I also resonate with her realization of Catholic vowed women as being "kept women;" we are so bound by law, so unable to act on our protest, even when we have one, especially in any communal sense. As I also resonate with "how uncomfortable it is for me...to really look compassionately at myself."

Conclusion

The 10 "tellings" contained in this chapter, distilled from longer narratives, proclaim both the presence of "original fire" in each woman and the details of where that fire has brought her in the present moment, whatever the circumstances of her particular life. In this way, they stand as testaments and can indeed be called personal "Scriptures," as Cora named them on her first reading of the transcripts.

Like scriptures, these stories present universal experiences manifested in the daily details of ordinary lives. Each woman articulates an inner strength larger than life as she navigates through clearly defined structures of constriction, oppression, and narrow thinking. The tellings could be proclaimed as Sacred Words, inviting all who hear them to search out their own "original fire" in response to the voices which proclaim it here.

I have also included brief reflections at the end of each story as to some of the specific ways in which the stories impact my own. In this case, I have sought out echoes of similarity and connection, rather than critique and dissonance. I have purposely highlighted "connected" rather than "separate" knowing (Belenky and Stanton, 2000 86), preferring to gather energies of connection rather than those of separation, in which all of us have lived for too long.

Finally, I have invited you, the reader, to notice your response to each story. Perhaps you would not be drawn to respond to all of them, but a word or a phrase, a spark or a light in one or more of them, might illumine your own story, whether you are a Catholic vowed woman or not. Indeed the responses of women outside the context of the vowed life are offered later in this book in order to highlight the universality of the inner struggles of women in a general sense.

CHAPTER V:
Fire Seed: My Own Transformative Journey

All her life she has been in love with the hope of telling utter truth... (W.S. Merwin, cited in Rich, 1991, back cover)

This study was undertaken in order to access the hidden ways in which transformation is happening to women, and especially religious women, in these days marking the end of renewal and the turning needed for transformation. It was also undertaken as a way to articulate the transformative energies that had begun to move in my own life. In the heart of this experience

Transformation may take many forms. Transformation is not only a world-changing re-visioning of self. It may also be a small, quiet revolution, an insight, a changed feeling - response to events in one's life or a new interpretation of an old belief which may seem modest in its impact. It may also be a felt-sense change which is not rationally explainable, a knowing that one is different because of encountering another's experience. Transformation simply means a non-reversible change in personality, however small or large. (Clements, et al. 1999, 193)

In such ways as these has my own story simmered with transformation throughout the entire process of this long writing. I have been telling of the insights, especially from chthonic (intuitive) sources and the small, quiet revolutions they engendered all the way through this document; however, in this chapter I will focus on how I responded to the same story prompts as my co-researchers. Following this, I will offer my response, as they did, several months after the initial telling. Then I will elucidate five specific areas in which I experience demonstrable inner change as a result of engaging in this inquiry.

Brenda's Telling

(I am 55 years old, and had lived religious life for 36 years at the time of this telling.)

My Original Fire links me to things, but it also separates me. It's a double-sided energy that causes me to see things differently from others and that compels me to speak what I see, sometimes in a public as well as a personal way.

My early life was shaped by a strange and unpredictable mixture of control and affection demonstrated by material gifts. That reality gave me the advantage of developing a rich inner life, because I found as many ways as possible to stay invisible. So— safety was an important preoccupation as a child, and I found more safety in the larger world than I did in the small and unpredictable world of my family. Both my parents struggled in a poor economy, with its accompanying pressures. My mother was focused most of all on my education, and somehow found the money to send me to the best school (it was thought) in the city at that time. Because she had taught me to read at the age of 3, I found a vibrant life in stories which allowed me to escape the sometimes chaotic world of my home. This ability to read beyond my years eventually led me to experience validation and affirmation in school, where achievement gave me the recognition I couldn't risk at home. Perhaps one of the first ways I felt what I'd now call "Original Fire" was around the age of 6 when we had to "learn off" catechism answers. "Why did God make you?" "To know, love and serve Him in this world so that you can be happy with Him in the next" actually made sense to me at 6; it felt like a compass or an inner focus for whatever happened. Because where I really blossomed was in school. The nuns who taught me were young, creative, vibrant women who didn't use physical punishment and who rewarded good grades and told stories and told us of their summer schools in the United States. Every Friday was a creative day given over entirely to art, embroidery and creative writing, which then went into a school newspaper, and music and drama, and even a movie! School was my haven, even throughout high school. As a teenager I delayed going home, and joined so many clubs that I didn't get home much before six every school day. By seven I was at my desk for three hours of study. So it's no wonder now that I joined the Congregation of the sisters who taught me. I believe they fanned the flame of that Original Fire in me, by seeing me just as I was and calling out my talents and then affirming them.

As a child I found my strongest connections in the devotional practices we were taught at school, especially visits to the Blessed Sacrament and the creative, personalized devotions of making spiritual bouquets for gifts. The Church formed a dependable and supportive structure which I did not find in my family. I also had a strong connection to the natural world. My father had property in a country place just outside the city where we lived every summer and fall. Most of his nine brothers and sisters also lived there, so we had a large gang of first cousins, all around the same age, who ran free and wild through the woods. I felt very safe and at home in the woods and still do, more than in any other setting. So my way of being in the world then was that in my immediate home setting I felt unsure and unseen for who I knew myself to be; I could find very little connection there. But the world outside—both school and nature—were both safe and nourishing.

Much of my adult life has been spent reconciling my inner fire with how I am seen in the outer world. I have always been very successful in the outer world— as a teacher, a counselor, a facilitator—and I receive a lot of affirmation. But the time came—all through my 40's, really— when I couldn't find a match inside with what people were saying to me on the outside. I would feel that the person people were affirming was not the one I knew on the inside. So I went on an intentional search for inner/outer congruence when I was about 47 or 48. This search was primarily sustained by my connection with the natural world. While most fully engaged in this process, I lived alone in a hundred-year-old log cabin on two miles of maple forest, with a pond which befriended and mirrored me. The healing came hard but true – a beginning which has only continued to deepen. In those years I began, for the first time, to hear my own voice and to know what I really thought about things and really longed for in my life. I believe that my Original Fire was fanned into a flame in this place, to which I gave the name "Soulweather Pond."

I'd been speaking out publicly before, but blindly, out of anger and need, without much thought or purpose. My experience with an eruption of priest-arrests for molesting children when I worked at an Archdiocese plunged me into an inner darkness: I now call that watershed experience "seeing into the dark heart of the Church." Of course, it was about losing a long support, a family really, which the Church was for me in my early years— I see that now. But that structure—and how I experienced it behaving in this circumstance, how there was no compassion for anyone, only a protection of the structure—that is something I can no longer identify with. It took many years, but when I finally allowed myself to internally disassociate from that structure, I felt a huge burden lifted from my shoulders. Such huge relief. My original fire burned me into that place, that truth.

So now I'd say that my Original Fire appears when I act against what is expected by both Church and Congregational authorities, and when I speak out publicly for unpopular causes. An example of that was when I wrote an article for the New Catholic Times last year questioning the Vatican Church's right to silence people, anybody really. This raised some anxieties. I sense that what I'm highlighting in this study might also. But I must speak it out, regardless.

I'm very aware that my choice to go with my Fire often means that I will lose a sense of belonging to something I don't necessarily want to lose, but I still must do it. Safety for me becomes a trap when the price of it is my own authenticity. I've lived with so many layers and layers of denial my whole life that I'm not sure I see an end to them, but nothing else is worth living now, as I get older. I have made some choices against the denial in the last few years choosing to see, for example, that my closest relationships have been with women for my entire life, but never seeing it and naming it as a pattern until now. And naming into awareness the hierarchical control of patriarchy in the Church that extends into women's religious communities is another. Even living from the view of feminism and women's spirituality means to sort out what might— even there—operate from controlling motives; it's still about stripping away layers of denial.

At the same time, I feel deeply bonded to people of good hearts whose desire to live out of an inclusive compassion is obvious from the way they live and act. This is not defined by Church or religious life but includes some of their members. I believe that my Original Fire helps me to be strong enough to hold opposites in tension until a new way of seeing breaks through. That's certainly what has happened around Church and religious life for me. I still strongly believe in the transforming power of women together, whatever form that takes.

Reading my story now, several months later, I am aware of a mixture of both apprehension and relief. I recognize the truth of my own words, truth that I have longed to speak aloud for many years, and I am simultaneously aware of the anxiety and discomfort such truth can evoke in others. While I feel the inner solidity of my own words, I also fear the separation and loss they might provoke: this has been a theme of my whole life. Yet, moving through this inquiry process has reformed me around what I have been calling my original fire: that inner prompting described by Istrati-Mulhern (1999): "for every step that I take along the Path - if I pay attention - I hear the faint whispers saying, 'YES', this way - even though this way is new territory... lonely...and not the same as many are walking."

Telling my story as part of the research process confronts me with all the ways I have long hidden my true perceptions. It gives me the intuitive and spiritual support needed to dig through the layers and layers of composting material to where the heat of original fire still burns, still survives a long smothering.

Gebara (2002) states that

personal storytelling helps us discover the complexity of influential psychological, social, economic, cultural and religious factors...this is not a matter of absolutizing individual experience but of showing how each person exists in relation with others, with the larger world, with the earth, and with the whole ecosystem (45).

In observing and recording my own story, not only the details of the past but the daily unfolding over a period of time, I have sometimes despaired at this complexity even as I learn from it. With Gebara, I have become aware of how "by telling my story I simultaneously reveal and conceal myself."(47).

Here, I offer what I know of my transformation thus far by identifying six shifts of consciousness I have been tracking throughout the duration of this process. These cover large areas of personal, relational, and spiritual growth evoked by the demands of the inquiry.

Vickers (2002) suggests that "writing of one's own life experiences is ... writing on the edge and without a safety net" (p. 608). This image gives form to my sensation as I reveal my inner feelings, thoughts, perceptions here—even when these demonstrate evidence of growth—or at least how we see growth in this progress oriented culture. Yet, through the insight which propels this writing: that is, that the personal life stories of Catholic vowed women are nowhere to be found except in the most spiritualized accounts filled with religiosity but not the real (e.g., Kaylin, 2000), I step into this emptiness with both trepidation and joy. Paying close attention to my inner process is strengthening my belief that we "engage in the communal participation of saving work through the continual re-writing of our lives" (Chopp, 1995, 77).

Identifying the Shifts

I have been experiencing inner transformation in six general areas which I will briefly describe here. I emphasize "inner" even though the word "transformation" implies this meaning, because what is being transformed is a set of structural inner beliefs, not necessarily (though this happens secondarily) visible outward behavior.

1. From Hiding to Revealing

During this study, I became acutely aware of a habit of hiding, especially from myself. I have several ways to do this: an inner "click" of closing off by placing my mind somewhere else; a refusal to look at the difficult aspects of something by focusing only on the positive or more comfortable aspects; and activity—especially tidying, cleaning and ordering space. I discovered that I hide my own pain from myself as well, and that I do this by withdrawing inside. I can trace readily this "hiding" propensity: As a small child hiding my real self was necessary when visibility brought physical and emotional danger. After entering religious life, hiding one's own thoughts and feelings was not only encouraged, but required; further, it was spiritualized; that is, justified by a belief that it was what God wanted. In those days we were taught that God wanted the complete annihilation of self—body, mind, spirit— in every way, in order to cultivate humility. It was not recognized then that most of us were too young to have formed a self at all. So the necessity of hiding, once a helpful ally, is now not only no longer needed, but is an actual hindrance in my present life, especially in comprehending the inner chaos that ensued when I came face to face with beliefs that no longer worked. An example of this shift would be that I believed, and quite absolutely, that I needed several hours almost every day for solitude and quiet. Yet, something in me was equally certain that I no longer wanted to live alone. Recognizing the conflict, I intentionally chose the new experience of living with a housemate who shared a similar commitment to the individuation process but from a more extraverted preference. In fact, we agreed to support one another's process in body, mind, spirit, and emotions. A stretch, indeed!

Being engaged in the study and practice of transformative learning during this time has surely enabled intellectual understanding of what is happening, but it has not relieved the feelings of terror, loss, isolation, and resistance that accompany this shift. My experience has followed Boyd's (1989) approach to transformative learning when he says: "The central purpose of a perspective transformation is to free the individual from his or her unconscious content and reified cultural norms and patterns that constrain the potential for self-actualization" (p. 459).

Many of my colleagues and family members would find it surprising, this insight about hiding. I am very good at it, practicing it for a lifetime. However, I am learning to reveal my inmost self *to myself* first of all, and cautiously to a few people. In order to do so, I walk a razor's edge of risk: so it feels. I inch my way through the old habits of fear and dark confusion. However, with awareness and intention, I am acting differently, choosing in small ways to reveal rather than to hide. This study is a large way to reveal my self, and writing it—through darkness—is healing the inner and outer split to which I referred in my telling.

2. *From Helping and Fixing to Bearing Witness*

I come from a family and a culture of small island thinking, a homogeneous population with very definite, right and wrong worldviews. Cause and effect, praise and blame are still readily assigned and reluctantly relinquished. Though I have always seen a larger picture, I also surveyed that larger world from a place of definite answers. Now I recognize the deep anxiety and uncertainty that lies at the heart of such fixed opinions. I see that the person holding such opinions—myself—is anxiously insecure to the same degree that she expresses the opposite.

One quality of such a static worldview is the impulse to fix, or at least to help, whatever one sees as "wrong," which usually means "different from the way I or we see it." (Peddigrew, personal communication, February, 2003). The Irish Catholic perspective, so steeped in fundamentalist, sin-focused Catholicism and simultaneous superstition, was the ambience of my growing up. Added to it was and still is an overlay of poverty, which grew into a negative victim mentality nevertheless paradoxically characterized by extreme hospitality that comes dangerously close to overstepping the personal boundaries of

107

others. It is difficult to argue with a generosity well beyond someone's means, yet the shadow side of such generosity tends to diminish its value. Other strands complicate its presence. The need to fix—everything or anything—for everyone, at least by telling how it should be, or the compulsion that I should somehow help, even when I can't or it isn't appropriate—these are ways in which I successfully escape knowing my self or the way the world really is, beyond my narrow interpretation.

In this process I am coming to terms with just how far my habit of fixing and helping has removed me from the reality of both myself and the world.

What is most helpful to stopping the helping and fixing compulsion is a deliberate focus on *bearing* witness to what is and realizing that my old tendency to fix and help keeps me from that bearing. I am learning to *bear*—and that is what it is—my own feelings, the feelings of others, the losses and grief and suffering around me, and my powerlessness to fix or even to help. Bearing my own feelings without helping or fixing means that I witness truth, rather than manipulate it for my own comfort. Yet, this is a hard struggle. The pattern is old and ingrained. It involves biting my automatic response-prone tongue, and dwelling in questions that have no answers. More than anything or anyone I've ever fixed or helped, bearing witness is an act of trust in the whole compassionate life energy at work in the world.

3. From Linear Time to Chthonic Time

The process of doing this study confronted me very uncomfortably with the limits of my habit of scheduling and organizing according to linear time. If I decide to do something tomorrow, for example, such as write for 3 hours in the morning, I am agitated if something interferes with the plan, whether it be external events or internal states of being. Surrender to the unpredictability inherent in an involved life has been a constant struggle, evoking anger when something external interferes and despair when my internal chaos refuses to conform to clock time. This struggle alone has allowed me to yield to the flow of life more readily, but still with an echo of the old disturbance.

Organic inquiry, which I've employed in this project, has been teaching me the significance of intuitive knowing by allowing me to consistently experience the deeper comprehending that makes itself known when I am able to suspend my schedule in order to paint, for example, or to walk or garden when I thought to read or write. I experience chthonic time as moving with the unexpected rather than denying or controlling it. In this constant struggle which has now become a challenge in ordinary life as well, I have found resonance with Morin and Kern's (1999) suggestion that "we should rather be led to experience the complementarity of different times, to reverse the domination of clock time...and to slow down in search of a new rhythm" (121).

4. From Outer Authority to Inner Authority

The most startling and prevalent shift in my own transformation is an awareness of how deeply and unconsciously I live according to external authority. At an age when—developmentally—people are finding their unique way in society, i.e., 17-30, I was submitting even more deeply to a religious hierarchy which required a spiritual relinquishing of three of the ways in which individuation naturally takes place. The traditional vows of celibacy, poverty, and obedience both negated and prevented intimate, loving relationships, personal responsibility for one's own financial functioning, and autonomy of life-decisions.

But the shaping of that negation began much earlier, when as a child, the first authority in my life in the person of my mother, was life-threatening. The Roman Catholic Church's requirement of weekly confession of sin from the age of 6 firmly ensconced the concept of a God who punishes, and that God was external to me. Without conscious intention, my life began to be shaped according to other's expectations because of the fear of punishment, and for many years as an adult I was quite unable to articulate any personal thought outside the system and through which I lived every detail of my life. Except one.

What could not be entirely repressed throughout nearly 50 years was my poetic voice, which I now recognize as a kind of intuitive knowing. From the age of 12, lines, words, whole original poems, and songs would announce themselves, and I would write them down. I have kept a journal since the age of 13, regularly having studied <u>Anne Frank: the Diary of a Young Girl</u> (Frank, 1952) in school. I see now that I identified with her imprisonment, though I wouldn't have named it that way then. I see that taking this voice seriously by writing it down kept alive the innermost voice of my soul which blossomed in its uniqueness only after becoming a doctoral student at California Institute of Integral Studies 3 years ago, at the age of 52.

Now I am becoming more adept at knowing what I believe and want and acting on that knowing even with the disapproval of others. How difficult it still is for me to disappoint others' expectations! However, I am well along this path, even with repetitive inner obstacles, of acting from the truth I encounter within myself. The fact that this learning is still new, requiring discernment and deliberation, is the reason why this chapter—my own story—carries fewer references and citations than any other chapter. I need to demonstrate that I can trust my own speaking without justifying it by an outer authority, even here. A few months ago while on a wilderness canoe trip, this sentence arose quite clearly inside, and I wrote it down: "I want no more authority in my life but wind, weather, and my own interior insight."

5. From Solitary Heroine to Interdependent Lover

For as long as I can remember, I thought of myself as essentially alone. Taught all my life by nuns and encountering very few enviable intimate relationships, I saw solitary service, even in religious community, as the highest calling, as closest to God. For most of my adult life I pursued and groomed myself in this image, and it was not until a few years ago that it shattered in brittle pieces all around me.

My shattering came because I met someone who reached in and opened the rusted shut door of my longing for connection. I had hidden this longing, even—perhaps especially—from myself, following my illusory dream of being the solitary heroine, which also fed the fixing and helping configuration described above. My world was shattered by this relationship, in which I encountered depths of myself and the other I could not have fathomed in any other way. An articulation of what happened for me, as I continued to distinguish women's experience from what I was told it should be, is found in Miller and Stiver (1997):

> If we observe women's lives carefully, without attempting to force our observations into pre-existing patterns, we discover that an inner sense of connection to others is development. Our fundamental notions of who we are - are not formed in the process of separation from others, but within the mutual interplay of relationships with others. In short, the goal is not for the individuals to grow out of relationships, but to grow into them. (21-23)

I saw my illusion for what it was: yet another imposed "ideal" that went directly against my inner nature.

Now, I am growing into interdependence in the large sense of love as, "excluding nothing, including everything" (hooks,

2000). I am growing into a sense of my place in the universe, which is all-important, and of no importance at all. I am growing into the concreteness of the universe, from a lifetime of abstract spiritual perception which dishonored my own (and everyone else's) physicality and promoted "the separation of humanity from the natural world" (Reason & Heron, 1997). I am experiencing firsthand what Keen (1983) points out with terrible clarity, that

> we will create a world that gives us evidence to support the metaphors by which we live. A warrior's world [or a heroine's] will be filled with allies and enemies and evidence of conspiracy and malevolent intent...a lover will discover [as I am discovering] increasing evidence that she is welcomed, graced, nurtured, and taken personally...that we are all bound together in a compassionate commonwealth. To become a lover is to risk exploring the logic of compassion (256).

6. From Disembodied to Earth Embodied

I am increasingly aware, over the course of this inquiry, of living from a deeper knowing that my "body is that piece of wilderness [I] carry around with me all the time, a living ecology which provides a home to many creatures and life events, which may be in balance or out of balance" (Reason, 1994, 13). I experience more and more often that the natural world is neither inanimate nor metaphor (Jensen, 2000), and that recognition is changing the way I live, relate, and pray. I am falling daily into deeper embodiment, sustained by a hunger to interact with nature and wilderness in wordless communion. From a body in which pain and joy were both paralyzed, a necessary early learning, I am slowly, and often with resistance, feeling cold and heat, physical limits which I no longer push through, and more moments of wordless connection with people and earthly seasons. This year I came to realize that I love snow with exhilaration and that trees feel like family. O'Murchu (2000) states "as creatures of the universe and inhabitants of planet Earth, there are, in the eyes of God, no reserved places" (26); this summarizes my sense of belonging truly to creation, not superior by way of being human, but simply a part of the whole web. It describes the sense in which I mean to speak of love: tender inclusion of all that exists, from the microcosm of my own self and the persons inhabiting my small world in relationship, to the incomprehensible range of cosmic creation. In these ways, my spirituality is both more grounded in the physical and more expansive in its vision than before.

In summary, who am I becoming? The truest response I find to that question is a recognition and affirmation of my own liminality according to O'Murchu (1999) when he defines liminality as a "threshold experience, [a calling] to those places apart where we are invited to provide a mirror-image in which the people can see reflected their own searchings, struggles, and hopes for a more meaningful existences" (18). I find further validation in O'Murchu's next line: I know I am one of "those called apart [who] are accountable first and foremost to the people (what Plato calls the 'polis'), and not to the church or to any formal religious system"(17).

The movement of my own life is toward inner authority. I have already come a long way from unquestioningly obeying the outer authority of Church and religious Congregation. I experience more of my life with the inner and outer congruence that I began to intentionally pursue nearly ten years ago. My "community" is those with whom I experience "mutual and meaningful participation" (Cox, 1999) and they are scattered all over the globe as well as in my original home. I feel quite clearly my connection with the long line of women who trust and act from their own Original Fire in resisting oppression wherever they find it, even in the Roman Catholic Church. I am able to do so because of those women, and the hundreds of thousands who have followed them and others throughout history, and who still do so, visible or invisible.

As for the traditional vows of celibacy, poverty, and obedience, in me they are evolving into new forms which carry the vibrant energy meant to characterize them from the beginning. Law-bound vows cannot do this, because their purpose is to bind and constrict. From the vow to not relate, which was what celibacy meant to me when I first vowed it at the age of 20, I have been moving towards a vow "to relate"(O'Murchu, 1999), which includes the whole earth in every manifestation. I have come to know my sexuality as a spiritual as well as a physical energy for both creativity and connectedness, and it is always seeking expression. Relating— whether it be to materials in art, people, groups, trees, ants, stars, stones—is a value that takes me far beyond the self-denial which originally defined my understanding of this vow.

From a vow of poverty, taught fundamentally as disdain for created things and therefore a denial of responsibility for creation, I am moving into what O'Murchu (1999) calls "mutual sustainability": awareness and embodiment of the "complementary relationship of growth and the environment... in a spirituality of non possessive owning"(67). Mutual sustainability as a value, not a vow, fuels the passion for justice on every level.

Finally, I claim the value of listening with a "radical and attentive openness to the deeper message and meaning of all that I am asked to attend to" (O'Murchu, 1999, 88). My experience with intuitive knowing in the writing of this book is, surprisingly, opening me to a whole new understanding of what deep listening means when it includes nonrational, unconscious influences on choice and behavior as found in Hollis (2003); Mindell (2002, 1993); MacEowan (2002); and Sams (1999), among others.

It is this quality of listening, this true inner guidance, that requires of me "mutual collaboration" with all whom I hear, in a nonhierarchical, inclusive mode that is opposite to my early understanding of the vow of obedience.

The vows which I publicly professed at the age of 20 have transfigured into constellations of values around which my life is daily lived. They are no longer recognizable in that first form, and they might not exactly fit prescribed canonical teaching on what they are supposed to look like. But those values now define my purpose and intention in the world and witness to the liminal calling that I have never felt so strongly. When I decided to begin this study at the age of 52, what fired my intention was a resonance with this passage from O'Murchu (1999):

> As people called to inhabit the liminal space, we realize that our vocation is to think the unthinkable, speak the unspeakable, bring to silence the raucous din of patriarchal verbiage and bring to word the subverted groans and imposed silence of the downtrodden and oppressed of our earth (47).

Today I find this passage even more significant than when I began this transformative process. The following poem, written on the Feast Day of my Congregation 6 months ago, tells me clearly where I now stand:

SEED

Mercy is a seed fallen from an empty husk.
The outer shell has cracked and split
as is its nature to do.
Let the husk go. Let it fall to fertilize the ground.
Care for the seed
falling into that same ground

115

where dormancy is but sleep
a gathering of life
until time
flowers it
into the world again.
But now
that seed is falling into the ground
falling into me
into my ground
into my winter.
I carry the seed of Mercy
in my own dark
wordless
soil.
Another sun will germinate me.
Another sky will water me.
Another love will fertilize me.
(Peddigrew, 2002)

("Mercy" is the name of my religious congregation of women)

That seed is my original fire. The poem can be interestingly read by substituting "fire" for the word "Mercy." As it has always been doing, to greater and lesser degrees, my original fire continues to smolder and flare, living the paradox of simultaneous seed and fruit.

I can summarize my personal experience with an image of "initiation" (Perera, 1981, 7). Indeed, having lived the shifts just described and having surrendered to intuitive darkness as the compass and pilot of this dissertation, I feel I have been initiated into the Mysteries of the Dark Feminine, in a way "not based upon passivity, but upon an active willingness to receive" (Perera, 13). The following paragraph summarizes best my experience of undertaking and following through with this study:

> The process of initiation in the esoteric and mystical traditions in the West involves exploring different modes of consciousness and rediscovering the experience of unity with nature and the cosmos that is inevitably lost through goal-directed development. This necessity—for those destined to it—forces us to go deep to reclaim modes of consciousness which are different from the secondary process levels the West has so well refined. It forces us to the affect-laden, magic dimension and archaic depths that are embodied, ecstatic, and transformative; these depths are pre-verbal, often pre-image, capable of taking us over and shaking us to the core" (13-14).

Which is exactly what happened.

C H A P T E R   V I :
What the Stories Say: Layers of Implication

The purpose of alchemy was not to make something out of nothing, but rather to fertilize and nurture the seed which was already present. Its processes did not actually create gold, but rather made the ever-present seed of gold grow and flourish.(Hall, 1977, 78)

The "tellings" presented in the two previous chapters contain many elements of the lives of Catholic vowed women that are not usually presented in a public way. They open us to the knowledge – and the truth – that the struggles of women may be the same wherever they are, and that the inner lives of nuns are not very different from their sisters in any other way of life. I have invited you to notice your own resonances, and the points in the stories that draw you into your own life. In this chapter, however, I will draw out some of the patterns and implications that I noted when taking the stories all together, and when I was steeped in the words – no, the lives – of these women. Next I will offer a way of seeing larger implications through the lens of transformative learning. Finally, I will present an image for moving from a linear approach – using a map - to an organic one: the metaphor of the wheel.

119

1. Common Threads

Eight commonalities run through most, if not all, of the stories. I did not set out to look for these, but the longer I spent with the stories themselves the more they asked to be written down. Given the communal nature of religious life, I offer these "threads" as they clustered around eight themes, and in random order.

- inner life...essential loneliness...God...devotion... mystical awareness outside time.. public and private... inner and outer dilemma.
- connection with the universe...natural world...Earth Mother..."let the lake be the lake"...trees...water...rocks... melting ice...fallen leaves...including and relating to everything in creation.
- serving the poor and disadvantaged as self-identity and validation... making the world a better place...helping somebody else.
- flowing with change...moving beyond what is...beyond whatever restricts, including institutional Church...finding doors in the walls...there is no one true perspective...
- longing for relationship...knowing self ...the mystery... intimacy with one other who sees me... my feminine self...the stars.
- Seeing the world differently from those around me... speaking truth to power...going against expectations of others...restlessness...dissent...resistance.
- disillusionment with Vatican II...imposition of hierarchical, patriarchal Church no longer tolerable... fire also gone out of institutionalized religious communities.
- "making visible the invisible"... flowering from within... no longer subject to external authorities.

Reflecting on these emerging threads brings me to a clearer perception about the inner life of Catholic vowed women than I had before I began this writing. I would still say that the form as we know it is moribund, devoid as it is of the usual form of new life; i.e., young members, and the appropriate maturing of current members. However, writing this chapter has brought me to see that, while this is true of that particular form, transformation is already happening, those old forms falling fast away, in the lives of women like the ones in this inquiry, who have found ways of staying connected to their original fire. I am reminded of MacEowen's (2002, 132) saying about stories that "no matter how much we look, we will not find a story outside ourselves. We have all been woven into this story. It is our story, because we are the story, and it continues to unfold." As the Roman Catholic Church in its present form refuses to acknowledge that, in the developed world, we are facing the death of a way of life - a way of life that nourished and sustained not only ourselves but the whole Church, and tries instead to address the diminishing number of nuns in the old and unquestioned ways of praying for vocations, running recruitment campaigns, advertising in Catholic newspapers, and silencing anyone who would disagree, *the hidden thread of transformation continues to unfold in subtle ways in the lives of Catholic vowed women who continue to discover their original fire.* As Sylvester (2000) publicly stated in an address to the Leadership Conference of Women Religious in the United States, "we are at an impasse with the Church that we love."

So there is more than what can be seen on the surface, and the "new" is coming forth through the dark passage of those who can go forward, *through* the ending that is in sight. This is the time of real faith, of leaping-in-the-dark faith with no certainties at all, from which large retirement funds will not protect us. This is the time when spirit, who "blows where it wills" (John 11:21) is tugging at our ankles, untying the knots of our old and safe moorings.

Merkle (1992, 219) articulated this challenge 10 years ago when she wrote: "It seems evident that religious congregations are at a crossroads...we need to ask ourselves if it is our inability to allow religion to function in a transformative manner in our congregations which is really calling into question the future of religious life."

Chittester (1995, 121) recognized that the activity of labor so fully characterizing Catholic vowed women was not enough; even professional education wasn't enough "if it fit us for particular skills...but neglects...dealing with the great questions of human life. The world needs thinkers who take thinking as a spiritual discipline. Anything else may well be denial practiced in the name of religion."

These reflections and those of the women whose stories are contained here call us to a new way of seeing, a new language that is more expressive of women's unique experience of life itself, an experience that is only political if the personal is valued. The language of conceptual frameworks – be they theological, sociological or ecclesiastical – cannot ground us, cannot give us any solid place in the world. They are, after all, only a layer of abstraction, and need to be seen as such. What grounds us first and foremost is claiming what it is to be a woman, in all dimensions; every other layer comes afterwards. This means living from body and emotions as well as mind and spirit, and recognizing that all of these are necessary to the fullness of who we are.

2. Larger Implications: the Lens of Transformation

The current understanding of transformation offers a fresh lens for seeing more deeply into what has been expressed in these stories. Transformative Learning theory holds several keys for understanding what is happening in religious life at this time, and could provide fresh language for articulating our experience.

Though Mezirow (2000) has been critiqued by some scholars for his rational and conscious approach to transformative learning (Boyd, 1989; Kegan, 2000b), I begin with his "disorienting dilemma" as the place for transformative reflection on religious life to begin. For religious communities, Vatican Council II was an intense disorienting dilemma, plunging Catholic vowed women into swift and sudden change. Subsequent Chapter meetings were exercises in "self-examination with feelings of anger, guilt and shame" (Mezirow, 2000, 22). But the lack of knowledge and experience in feeling emotions and critiquing that was characteristic of vowed women in 1965 meant that the next two elements of Mezirow's transformative unfolding did not take place: "a critical assessment of assumptions" and "recognition that one's discontent and the process of transformation are shared." Instead, many groups moved immediately to "an exploration of new roles, relationships, and actions," and to "planning a course of action" without examining assumptions on any level or recognizing the important role of discontent and critical reflection as transformative. This move reflects the dominant intellectual and religious preference of Catholic vowed women at the time of Vatican II; that is, a decided negation of any place for emotions and body-knowing in ordinary life, and especially in decision-making. In this regard, vowed religious women reflected the more general characteristic of most women during that time. Certainly, Hegel's (Kegan, 2000b) description of spirit as "never at rest but always engaged in ever progressive motion, in giving itself new form" would be outside the awareness of vowed women.

"Renewal" was and is far from balanced in the sense of an integral approach to transformative learning. One reason for this could be that a significant number of women entered communities before the age of 20 and were subsequently "made up by the values and expectations of their surround (family, friends, community, culture), uncritically internalized, and with

123

which they became identified" (Kegan 2000b, 61). Despite this fact, and as I hope I am showing in this book, some members were nonetheless still able to shift "from a socialized to a self-authoring epistemology" (Kegan, 2000b, 65).

Brookfield (2000) offers a transformative learning approach that would help Catholic vowed women to comprehend more fully their present dilemma. He suggests using both objective and subjective reframing:

> Objective reframing focuses on learners doing a critical analysis of the concepts, beliefs, feelings or actions communicated to them, or pausing to examine assumptions about the ways problems or actions have been framed. Subjective reframing emphasizes critical analysis of the psychological or cultural assumptions that are specific reasons for one's conceptual and psychological limitations (131).

Taken together, these two approaches would offer a whole and integrated reflection on what has been happening in religious life since Vatican II.

Taylor (1998) analyzes three other interpretations of Transformative Learning that might be helpful in applying this framework—in its many variations—to religious life. Boyd (1989): "Transformation as Individuation;" Freire (1970): "Transformation as Social Emancipation," and Saavedra's (1996) identification of conditions essential for transformative learning in a group setting. Both Taylor himself and Cranton (1994) offer practical exercises for stimulating critical self-reflection and supporting transformative learning.

Finally, O'Sullivan (1999), writing about transformative learning within an ecological and planetary context, uses images from the new physics to describe in that language the historical moment in which we find ourselves in religious life: "If the fluctuations of the system reach a critical level, the system becomes sufficiently turbulent so that the old connecting points no longer work; the system transforms itself into a higher order, one with new and different connection points" (209).

To these I add my own experience of transformative learning, written in my academic journal over a year ago, and summarizing here the relevance that this framework might offer for vowed religious women, and all women, at this time:

> Transformative Learning is the tipping point from intellectual prowess and organizational predictability and control into the realm of mystery and spirit. This language ("mystery and spirit") is not often used in this discipline, but anyone who walks through a disorienting dilemma to its end—transformation—inevitably comes to the place of stepping into the Unknown, completely and utterly devoid of ground and light – and trusting in raw faith that this is not an end, but a beginning. (Peddigrew, 2000)

Conclusion: from outer to inner authority

The 11 stories in this book point to "new and different connection points" and to the "realm of mystery and spirit" for Catholic vowed women. Our new connection points widen our experience to include that of many women in North American culture having nothing to do with Catholic religious life and separate us from many with whom we would be connected in the old forms (i.e., by Canon Law). The stories told here illustrate some individual women's natural unfolding into new shifts of consciousness after the major one was made: that of acting from

125

inner authority rather than always conforming to outer authority. The stories easily make clear in every case that our ways of being in the world were dramatically and permanently altered by following from within. They demonstrate that – beneath all the abstract ways that women's vowed religious life is identified – lies the personal, universal, concrete and spiritual reality of women-being-women. Which is to say, women finding ways to live from their inner fire, whether those ways be visible or not.

CHAPTER VII:
Shifting the Metaphor: from Linear Map to Organic Wheel

You will find more things in the midst of the forest than in books. The trees and the rocks will teach you what you cannot learn from any master. (St. Bernard of Clairvaux, 1153)

There is an easily demonstrable phenomenon in recent history that sudden and radical shifts of collective perception can take place within a few years, or within one generation. One blatant example of this is how North American society moved from a promotion of smoking as a sign of maturity to near persecution of smokers, sometimes threatening to refuse them health care if their disease is nicotine-related. This amazing difference happened within relatively few years. In the same but a much less public way, a change has begun to happen within the perception of those who used to see religious life as simply going on the way they always lived it and remembered it. This change was first highlighted in a study by Nygren and Uteritis (1992) in which "stages" of religious life were charted in congruence with natural cycles of evolutionary movement. In terms of metaphor, an apt image would be that of shifting from seeing the present/future as a linear, progressive reality to living it from the perspective of a cyclical, organic approach. In other words, we are moving from following a map to walking a wheel.

Heron (1998, 86) states

a sound map will not give an authoritative account of the predetermined return route to the divine. Rather, it will modestly pre-suppose that what is going on in our cosmos is an undetermined, innovative process of divine becoming in which we are all immersed.

Our attempts at mapmaking, however, emphasize accuracy of detail and predictability. A map's purpose contains a linear goal: to move from point A to point B with the least possible number of unknown obstacles. Heron's description is not the usual way a map is thought of, and yet it serves as a paradoxical reminder of our tendency to look for an "authoritative account of the pre-determined return route to the divine." In a cosmos where "what is going on...is an undetermined, innovative process of divine becoming in which we are all immersed," maps as we usually engage them are questionable entertainments, pulling us into our tendency to grasp at a possibility of certainty, no matter how illusory.

Maps are also mental models, having little to do with the whole experience of a journey in the engagement of all the senses. Such maps are out of date as soon as a new sign is added or removed; a house built or destroyed; or, in the case of "sacred" maps, a new, original experience calling an older one into question. Organizations of every kind attempt to create maps of predictability; institutions, Churches included, are well known for this endeavor. But "the maps they gave us were out of date by years" (Rich, 1984, 242). We live in a time when maps become out of date almost as soon as they are made.

The need for certainty and predictability in Church and religious life has already been challenged. O'Murchu (2000, 15) asks,

> Why are we afraid to die to our past traditions? Why do they have to last forever? Why do we consider so many of them to be above the provisional nature of all human inventions? Why not seek to outgrow it, even if that means ultimately abandoning it?

Even as early as 1994 (4) Fiand was positing:

> We have enabled emancipation and by so doing may have...ministered ourselves out of a way of life. We may have reached the end of the purpose for our founding. Could it be that, for whatever reason, we are not able to foster the communities necessary for adult growth and maturation, or even for the flourishing of new life?

These questions have helped me to articulate my own real query— no, belief—about where we are now in the unfolding story of religious life. While surveying relevant writings for this study, I experienced a moment of intuitive knowing that was expressed inside me visibly as a "map" of sorts(see Appendix C). This diagram seemed at the time (March, 2002) to contain as complete a vision of religious life as possible, within a transformative paradigm. It refers to the broad lines of past, present and future. It offers the metaphor of "transformative cocoon" for the present and emphasizes as much of the unknowable as the knowable for the future. Drawing out this map gave me a satisfying sense of completion, as maps are meant to do. And therein lies the illusion.

By now, this map is already "out of date, by years," not so much in its content, which remains for the most part true and helpful even in its incompleteness, but by showing me so completely the limits of "map" as metaphor.

I cannot identify the exact moment of realizing that the metaphor of "wheel" rather than "map" is more realistically reflective of the emerging expression of religious life for Catholic vowed women, but it was around the time that I heard about an effort at recruitment of new members being made in North American Communities. Having been Director of Initial Formation for my own Congregation from 1979-1984, and leaving that work over a disagreement with my leadership over the issue of recruitment, I remain sensitive to that endeavor. When I inquired further into this new campaign, I was doubly discouraged by the modes and documents being employed: not only were they written in the language of the early 80's, but some of the actual documents written during those years (I was one of the writers) were being reproduced word for word. Pondering why and how this state of affairs could come about now, I came to some insights that shifted me into the metaphor of the wheel and away from a linear "map" representation.

To think about religious communities (or any organization) in a linear way is to assume (a) continual forward movement and (b) that members of the organization are responsible for that forward movement. Linear development is achieved by goals and strategies and planned change. This is the language of renewal, not of transformation.

Inviting as those documents and plans may be (and no one is better at producing well-written, even charismatic, documents than communities of Catholic vowed women), they are created without reference to body, emotions, and the spirit of change that is unpredictable by its very nature. As such, they remain in the intellectual realm, without effecting much real change. Even more tragic is the guilt and frustration of members—especially leadership and formation personnel—who subsequently act from the belief that "it's up to us to make this happen," or "if we only pray harder, they will come." Years of this have changed nothing. Numerical diminishment (see statistics in chapter II) continues and accelerates.

One significant implication of this inquiry is that the degree to which Catholic vowed women have been cut off from the flow of life—by the vows themselves—by what O'Murchu (1999) calls the excessive "institutionalization and domestication" of those vows; to that degree, the groups cannot change *as groups*. This is the case even though a few individual members, for example, the co-researchers in this inquiry, are able to attend to their own transformation apart from institutional overlays.

The Wheel: a different language

If the language of the map is that of linear time and planned renewal, then the language of the wheel is one of charismatic time (Heron, 1999) and *surrendering to* rather than *planning for* transformation. The wheel as life metaphor connects us to cycles, dispelling the illusion of sustained and sustainable increase; it includes the multidimensional nature of what it means to live either individually or communally, and it offers a framework for seeing our place within the larger energies moving the cosmos. Living within the wheel exposes the small-sightedness of intellectual dominance alone, which buried the fire of religious communities for decades, and even now assures the imbalances that prevent transformation from taking place.

The image of "Wheel" is traceable as a metaphor for the cycle of life in many traditions. It is more dominant in earth-based traditions such as those of aboriginal peoples (LaChapelle, 1998; Reagan, 1994) and pre-Christian Celts (McCoy, 1998, MacEowen, 2007), but the image of wheel is also quite prominent in the mystical illuminations of Hildegard of Bingen (c.1148)

(Hildegard, 1986/1995) and even in the writings of the Old Testament prophet Ezechiel (1:15-21, 10:9-14). In all cases, the wheel symbolizes a way to flow with creative, Divine Energy rather than to direct and control that energy. The wheel image is a reminder that "we can't direct living things" (Wheatley, 1996).

My own engagement with the wheel is yet another example of how intuitive knowing has directed my learning and brought me, over the past 2 years, to the insight which is now the clearest outcome and implication of this study. In the autumn of 2000 I found myself reluctant to begin the semester of study, without knowing why. Instead, I felt compelled to research and then to build a Medicine Wheel in our backyard, an activity which took several days. Every one of those days I struggled with whether I was avoiding writing by undertaking this project. Initially, I was consciously using Arrien's (1993) Fourfold Way as a framework; I had adopted it as a spiritual practice several years before. But as the activities of building the wheel unfolded, I began to see everything in fours, and actually began a list, some of which follows:

-body, mind, spirit, emotions
-show up/pay attention/tell truth without blame
or judgment, let go of outcome (Arrien, 1993, 14)

-earth, air, water, fire
-north, south, east, west
-Kolb's (1983) four learning styles

-love, beauty, right action, knowledge (Reason, 1993, 143), on what constitutes Sacred Science

-experience, representation, understanding, action (Reason's 1993 "four aspects of sacred inquiry")

-affective, imaginal, conceptual, practical (Heron's 1994
primary modes of functioning)

-Torbet's four territories of human experience
(Torbet, 1991, 56)

-the good, the true, the one, the beautiful (Hillman, 1999, 67)

-four steps of empathic listening (O'Neil, 1999, 5)

-Wilbur's (2000) Quadrant Theory:
Intentional, Behavioural, Social, Cultural. (89)

The numinosity of "fours"—and this list is just the briefest of beginnings—was a puzzling feature of that semester's learning until I realized that "four" is about equilibrium, not balance. The equilibrium of fours is about cycling through seasons, and the Medicine Wheel as a form carries the capacity to contain that equilibrium. I felt the wheel calling me to this awareness in my own life in ways I was unable to perceive before that time. As I surrendered to those parts of my own "wheel" least developed (i.e., body and emotions) I entered a period of what could be called "spiritual initiation" (Sams, 1999) in which I literally temporarily lost my ability to see and was unable to engage in familiar activities – such as reading and driving - for several months. Needs of body and emotions became primary, out of proportion, as had indeed those of mind and spirit been for most of my life. Precarious and frightening as that time was, I also trusted that it was taking me somewhere I needed to be.

Now I see that this personal, intuitive experience mirrors what I have been gathering about Catholic vowed women's communities throughout the course of this inquiry.

Conclusion: Where we Might Be Now

The primary goal of this study is transformation instead of information, and individual transformation as well as collective. Ettling (1998, 123), one of the originators of organic inquiry, suggests that "organic research studies, so far, tend to be more feminine, grounded, and focused toward offering ways of interpreting and improving daily life or social reality". It is from this understanding of an organic approach to this study that I offer here some thoughts that could suggest fresh ways of "interpreting and improving" the daily life and social reality of communities of Catholic vowed women. Pursuing this line of thinking, I write from a leaning towards "the personal being universal" (Anderson, 1998). By gathering implications through this transformative frame, I also see the possibility of transformation through narrative theology according to Chopp (1995); Goldberg (1982) and Stroup (1981), whose understanding of the role of stories is that "each telling brings new elements and joins different elements together in the advancing saga of telling the important stories of one's life, or the important stories of one's community, tribe, or people" (Braud and Anderson, 1998). The primacy of "community," in all its current diversity of interpretation in the lives of Catholic vowed women, motivates me to reflect on how the stories here might shed some light on the present predicament of the communities themselves. I echo a well-known feminist phrase as a purpose of this chapter: "Naming is power" (Hunt, 2002). And perhaps the most significant voice on this power of story comes from Christina Baldwin (2005) when she writes "Something is happening in the power and practice of story: In the midst of overwhelming noise and distraction, the voice of story is calling us to remember our true selves."

So—after this circular, wandering, web-like exploration— who are we as women among women, as human beings struggling with other human beings? Who are we without religious and canonical trappings?

The stories and findings of this inquiry, focused on an inner experience rather than external definition, indicate a clear congruence of the lives of Catholic vowed women with women in the larger population. This matching becomes eminently clear in the next chapter, "Ripples of Transformation," which shows that—just as women in a general sense cannot be defined by marriage or other cultural norms—Catholic vowed women cannot be defined by ecclesiastical prescription or canon law. Such definitions exist—in fact, are used culturally to depict nuns more than any other description—but the tellings in Chapter IV indicate that these storytellers find little inner connection with such definitions. In fact, the stories show them living their essence from an inner place—what I call their "original fire"—which has meant often acting in opposition to those very definitions while keeping that opposition hidden in a public sense.

Women Speaking Their Own Truth: the Difficulties

Gilligan (1982) and Rich (2001) write eloquently of the difficulty women have in speaking their own truth. Gilligan shows in her eloquent study that

> choices not to speak are often well-intentioned and psychologically protective, motivated by concern for people's feelings and by an awareness of the realities of one's own and others' lives. And yet, by restricting their voices, many women are wittingly or unwittingly perpetuating a male-voiced civilization and an order of living that is founded on disconnection from women (153).

Rich writes even more concretely and starkly about how women have been trained to lie as a result of the need for survival and belonging in a male culture:

> We have been expected to lie with our bodies: to bleach, redden, unkink or curl our hair, pluck eyebrows, shave armpits, wear padding in various places or lace ourselves, take little steps, glaze finger and toenails, wear clothes that emphasized our helplessness. We have been required to tell different lies at different times, depending on what the men of the time needed to hear (33-34).

The stories begin to demonstrate that these realities still exist, but they also show something else: That the voices are beginning to speak. That the silences are being broken. That a new language, a woman's language, is emerging in the understories of how we see women living, the choices they make in fierce fidelity to the original fire of their inner authority. Speaking one's truth often sounds attractive in the idea, but daunting in the doing of it, as our storytellers Mary and Grey Jay make particularly plain in their narratives. Gilligan offers reasons:

> And then I will remember how it felt to speak when there was no resonance, how it was when I began writing, how it still is for many people...speaking depends on listening and being heard; it is an intensely relational act (1982, 172).

Mary's Telling echoes Gilligan's observation when she shares how hard it often is when she speaks and the room goes into silence, and when she leaves there is murmuring. This lack of resonance, this "undermining of one another's reality for the sake of expediency" (Rich, 2001, 35), raises a challenge to all women: *that we practice hearing one another without that undermining one another, which really means without undermining ourselves.*

Another major area in which Catholic vowed women echo women's dilemma and highlight the need for reflective change is the area of "the angel in the house—the woman who acts and speaks only for others—abdicating her right to speak and essentially disappearing both from relationship and responsibility" (Gilligan, 1982, 14). While many women are engaged in breaking out of this role by studying and working outside the home, Catholic vowed women were seen and saw ourselves—many still do—as the servants of the Church, which for many still exclusively means the male hierarchy. In common parlance, the term used for nuns was often "cheap labor." The depth of this belief was borne out when many priests and Bishops expressed strong indignation at the move by some Catholic vowed women to ask for just wages according to their education and culture. I was involved in this movement and experienced it personally. I also see it resonating with the general reluctance in Western culture to enforce equal pay for equal work, and to give monetary value to women's work in the home.

This study affirms that—beneath the religious trappings and cultural stereotypes—Catholic vowed women are women first and foremost, struggling with the dilemmas of women everywhere. Like women everywhere, our struggle is against patriarchal parameters and hierarchical authority that places no value on relationship, on interconnections on any level except that which corroborates the authority. As the "tellings" clearly announce, our "original fire" is the voice of each woman who dares to "fiercely speak truth to power", as Grey Jay sees her vocation now.

Conclusion: Catalyst and Crucible

Historically, the deepest desire of Catholic vowed women has been to be engaged with the struggle of all human beings. Our organizations were founded for this purpose alone, in each one's historical time and place. But from the beginning, our organizations were also tethered to the Vatican Church and canon law, contained by them in the same ways that women are contained by cultural norms and societal expectations, except with the additional overlay of religious power. Recognizing the dying of our way of life as I have been noting throughout this inquiry raises the question as to whether our vital essence, our original fire, has lost its energy to that tethering.

I consider it beyond the scope of this book to do more than highlight the questions that arise from the silences of Catholic vowed women. However, I also consider this document to be a beginning, a catalyst for transformation in my intention to facilitate its larger unfolding among women, of which Catholic vowed women are a small but significant strand.

Let this study be not only a catalyst for calling forth the voices and the languages of women, but a crucible for the faithful work that emerges after we have spoken. It is not enough to critique patriarchy or to define ourselves by acting against it. *We need a new alphabet altogether, an original articulation of our most genuine longing and perception of the world* that will then enable us to make changes towards inclusion and liberation for all. Catholic vowed women have always been part of this enterprise. As hooks (2002, 15) states so succinctly: "Women, along with the culture as a whole, need constructive visions of redemptive love. We need to return to love and proclaim its transformative power.

CHAPTER VIII:
Rippling Outward: Women Respond in Their Own Voices

Life is no passing memory of what has been
Nor the remaining pages of a great book
Waiting to be read.
It is the opening of eyes long closed
It is the vision of far-off things
Seen for the silence they hold
It is the heart after years of secret conversing
Speaking out loud in the clear air.
(David Whyte, 1987)

When it comes to a cultural perception of women who most visibly conform to external authority, "nuns" – Catholic vowed women – would be among the first groups to be named to that dubious category. That was one of the reasons I chose these women for this study, suspecting that something other than the usual external definitions was at work, fueling the creative life of service I saw happening wherever nuns lived and worked. If their "original fire" could survive such stricture, then it was truly hopeful for women everywhere. One of the respondents in this chapter put it this way: "It's as though the struggle of all women to escape from patriarchal systems of social arrangements is

139

crystallized in vowed women. The confining structures are so blatant and more invasive than for other women." (Jean)

After the formal study which is the foundation of this book was completed, I began to invite other women to read it for themselves. Specifically, I wanted to know how women who had no experience of being in the vowed religious life, or who were not even Catholic, might respond to the material, especially the stories, and how those stories might interface with their own lives. Looking back, I see now that I was hoping that women outside the structures might actually see through the overlays of Church and the language of religious life to the shared soul of being woman. Not only was I not disappointed, I was somewhat astounded, even overwhelmed in a few cases, with the connections that were made. The women who speak their own responses in this chapter are listed at the end, with a brief biographic description. The names given there are pseudonyms, and their words are printed with permission.

I chose women who were interested in the study, first of all, not seeking them out, but simply saying "yes" to each one's expressed desire to read the original document. When I gave them the copy, I then asked if they would give me, in return, two or three sentences in response to four questions. These are:

1. What words would you use to describe your inner experience of reading this document?
2. What did you resonate with or feel disturbed/ repelled by?
3. Describe any other feelings...surprises...responses.
4. What effects might this document have on how you interact in the world?

My own biggest surprise was the length and depth of each response. Not one replied with two or three sentences. In one case, a woman was so stirred that she got up soon after midnight and wrote through to morning, sending me 6000 words! Another sent 10 pages, allowing her response to send her spiraling into her own questions, long denied. How most of the women went immediately to the core issue, both in the nuns' stories and in their own lives, without being sidetracked in the details of form, was encouraging to me. From follow-up conversations with some of the respondents, I see steps taken and lives changed in ways that come directly from their encounter with this material. Thus transformation happens. But let these women speak for themselves, in their own words.

1. Inner Experiences of Reading

I was moved by the universal struggle for all women to find their voices. I felt the sense of isolation, pain and rejection that each woman has suffered...and that it is each woman's individual suffering and individual transformation that will heal the world. I was moved by the courage of each woman who chose to stand outside collective values and stand in her own truth. (Marie)

I identified most with one sentence spoken by Grace:"I'm beginning to consider the possibility that there is nothing wrong with me." Some of us need to choose that sentence as a mantra and be required to say it in moments of self-doubt, despair, and low levels of courage. (Jean)

"What moved me most was the honest truth of how it has been in religious life. To see it written down moved me to tears." (Nancy)

*I felt the power of knowing that this writing echoed so well "women's dilemma." It haunted me, because I have experienced most of the same feelings throughout my life. What moved me was **how much** I could identify with it...all the stories, and how similar are the struggles of Catholic vowed women and particularly married women. This penetrated me. (Barbara)*

I was profoundly moved by the sheer honesty of the tellings. (Carmel)

I was overwhelmed by the stirrings of authenticity in women's lives. (Cate)

I experienced that these women's stories caused me to think about my own original fire. (Rachel)

Here is my inner experience of reading: I was intellectually stimulated, surprised, anxious, curious, provoked, saddened, hopeful. (Frances)

My inner experience was excitement and relief. We are all the same, quaking and naked behind our chosen shields...while we fight off the miserable truth. I feel a compelling connection to the tellers, maybe because nuns have played such a significant and nurturing role in my young life, and partly because I share their struggles and contradictions. (Sarah)

2. Resonances and Disturbances

This line: "Safety for me becomes a trap when the price is my own authenticity." Wow! This could be a subtitle for everyone's book! (Sarah)

I resonated with the self-realization that choosing to care for others and devote a large part of my life to being the best that I can be in that caring role can also oppress self-needs, desires, wants, etc., and that isn't ok. I felt repelled and angered by the acknowledgment of the rape of Catholic vowed women and children and startled by the covering up. (Frances)

The fear of separation and loss resonates deeply within me as I make a parallel journey and it is this revelation and vulnerability that connects me to the other women that I know I am not wandering out into the wilderness alone. (Marie)

Who am I when I stand alone? (Rachel)

I am upset and shaken by the system that treats women as vows alone...(Jane)

I am not disturbed but there is a disturbance within me...some of it confirms my own suspicions...my belief in the hierarchical church left me years ago or I left it...(Carmel)

What disturbs me is not anything I don't already know, but because it is so incomprehensible...that sexual, physical, psychological abuse is so covered up and denied...(Barbara)

Religious women have watered their roots until they have become so saturated they are beginning to die. I resonate with the truth of this whole document. (Nancy)

How difficult it must be for vowed women to disentangle themselves from the strait-jacket of institutional thought as well as the effects of language that acts as a chastity belt for mind and emotions. (Jean)

3. Other Feelings and Surprises

I share the tellers' struggles and contradictions: search for truth, for self-affirmation, for meaning as well as for external validation. We all want to be seen and accepted among the chosen even as we resent them...I am also surprised to encounter the level of sharing which you offer in this paper, Brenda...(Sarah)

I felt a sense of my own vulnerability in reaction to reading secret and private thoughts of the participants. I felt accepted and "let in" to the world of older wiser women and united and connected to all these women! A BIG surprise: Motherhood is oppressive. That jolted me. Mothering the self may not be as oppressive, but mothering/devotion to children can be. (Frances)

I was shocked by the degree of cruelty, mental and physical endured by all the women. I was saddened by the tales of contempt for the body that was so pervasive in the culture of religious life. This lifts the veil of illusion around it...I am struck by the realization that perhaps the greatest poverty among vowed religious women has been their own sense of self, which seems to have been shorn from their consciousness by the patriarchy just as surely as their hair was shorn before taking the veil. The term "kept woman" and the reality of it hit a hot spot and my original fire flamed with rage! (Marie)

*I was surprised to remember my own beginning life **outside** my group, not bound as strongly to family and group, in fact feeling more outside than inside...but the tellings unite me with women and deep inquiry that smolders and sparks...the original fire! (Cate)*

I am overpowered by the honesty of the stories and the women who told them...also glad that someone else sees not a hierarchical trinity but a circle. (Jane)

I am surprised by the putting of words onto this whole experience. I have a sense of the whole document "being birthed." It's as though you have developed a new vocabulary and language and, in fact, I think you have. I am surprised too at my failure, prior to reading this thesis, to see the connection between "imposed renewal" of Vatican II and the failure which is probably inherent in such an imposition. (Carmel)

Why were priests and nuns denied the warmth and comfort of close friends and immediate family? This is inhumane. To deny any physical or psychological knowledge, to consider the body and all its functions sinful, to forbid one-to-one friendships and deem them sinful is definitely disturbing to me. It is not only upsetting; it shakes my beliefs and definitely causes me to question. What surprises me the most is the number of women who have suppressed their inner fire by not questioning or refusing to discuss the validity of celibacy, money, and above all autonomy. It is astonishing that even after Vatican II, the silence of Catholic vowed women has barely been broken. This silence echoes the general silence of all women all over the globe to some degree. (Barbara)

To keep private the first scientific study on the sexual abuse of nuns in North America disturbed me most. This is morally wrong: they should be published. (Nancy)

To my knowledge, the Catholic hierarchy hasn't much bothered to "pretty up" its requirements. So the fact that a vowed woman is able to discover the heat of original fire and use it to illuminate her own spiritual path is remarkable. (Jean)

4. Different in the World

In recent years I've closed the book on personal growth. It doesn't matter why. What matters is that I need to change that now. Thanks for the kick in the butt.

She comes
circling my truth
like some nesting bird
to home.

I brace myself as she finds me.

Magnet to iron
She holds me to my pain;
Earth to her fire
I crumble.   (Sarah)

I feel it is time to take action! To take my thoughts (MY THOUGHTS!!!) and to awaken that part of me that has been hiding...to awaken my soul with loving kindness and see what comes. I need to take care of myself in relationship to my husband and to be less reactive to his needs for caring and support – I don't want to repeat the queen/king hierarchy I saw growing up – I want to be equal – giving and receiving love and support for personal growth and development. I LOVE WOMEN. I am connected to all women...I am part of a SISTERHOOD! I am supported...(Frances)

My fire burns brightly now, from the inside, not the outside. Before my break with the institutional church, I struggled to fan the dying embers that generated no energy. I realize now that the institution had all but snuffed out the fire of my sexuality, creativity and individuality, and the questions I so wanted to live. This fire eventually died and transformed when I left the institution. It has roared into life in the poetry I have started to write, the sexuality that is renewing in my relationship with my husband and in the values that I choose to live by that fall outside the collective. My fire burns with others though perhaps in a different camp. Maybe we need to send smoke signals to each other...make a pathway through the woods to connect our camps and tell the stories to each other around a campfire. The healing is in the telling and in the stories being received and reverenced. (Marie)

The ordinary yet tender inquiries of women whom I don't know and the manual of words in front of me give value in my world to the ordinary magic experience of being here in a body with a tender heart and the longing to be fully here. (Cate)

So rather than breaking away from an institution or a confining relationship I need to break away from my own self-image which had everything to do with how others perceived me and ended up affecting my emotional and physical health. Now I am working at fanning my Original Fire in the new context of learning about and caring for myself. (Rachel)

I realized that I was not fanning my flame. I had put the flame in a glass jar to stop it from going out in the storm. The clouds have just passed but I forgot I had put my flame in a jar. Now, rather than lift the flame out of the jar I will just gently remove the jar and set it down somewhere behind a tree – just in case I ever need it again.

I want to run outside and give this thesis to a number of women I know, and to one man in particular who is struggling with his religious congregation...but really I have been asking myself "what was the original fire of my marriage, have we remained true to it, how have we distorted it, what have we done to the original fire in each of us and to the fire of that commitment? My husband has been observing me (as only he can!) reading this thesis, I know he sees me coming down the track towards him. It is still too soon for me to try to tell him of my response to my reading, but a document like this cannot be read and left there. (Carmel)

While reading this dissertation I definitely recognized my individuation. Through the years, my Original Fire forced me to voice and comment even if at first I didn't do anything about it. In the last few years this fire turned into a roaring inferno that I could not suppress or ignore any longer, whatever the consequences. Now I have an identity once again, one other than being someone's wife or mother! As a woman and as a mother, I am making sure to teach my daughters accordingly in order to bring about change for women...My love for God and my faith has not changed very much since reading this dissertation. However my lack of faith in the Catholic Church has solidified somewhat. (Barbara)

Unless we learn that dreadful truth,
That each of us,
Each solitary, imperfect soul
Matters profoundly to the universe,
Then we will blindly stumble
Along another's path
with another's map. (Jean)

Biographical Descriptions

Barbara is a middle-aged mother of two daughters, raised in an Italian-Canadian family. She is an avid reader and gardener, and since reading the dissertation is becoming a writer.

Carmel is a mother and grandmother, singer and writer, and a faculty member for a Catholic theological college. She is presently pursuing a Masters' degree.

Cate is a mother of two grown daughters, a naturopath, outdoorswoman and explorer of divine mysteries in a variety of traditions.

Frances is a mother of twin boys under ten, a homeopath and presently studying to become a spiritual therapist. She is of the Jewish tradition and enjoys the outdoors with her family.

Jane is a mother of two daughters, pursuing a Master's degree in Theology and increasingly discovering her talents and abilities, now that her daughters are grown.

Jean is a recent widow, mother and grandmother, and former Catholic who is returning to her practice as a family therapist, adding in the spiritual and transformative dimensions. She loves the outdoors and treasures her Irish Wolfhounds.

Marie is a mother of three boys and works in the Catholic educational system.

Nancy is a Catholic vowed woman who is glad to see what was written and hopes for the transformation of women's vowed life.

Rachel is a mother of two adult sons and a faithful Christian of a protestant denomination. She is an avid homemaker and traveler.

Sarah presently makes her living as an artist and grew up in the Catholic tradition. She has been a nurse, a counselor, and an activist for women's rights.

The power of these women's voices leaps out of the pages. Read aloud, they resound as proclamations of freedom. Through reading the stories spoken by Catholic vowed women earlier in this book, these women encountered their own lives. They were able to see through the outer form to the inner essence: i.e., the original fire that is the soul of each woman, and every woman. Each woman's life changed – some more subtly than others – by recognizing the inner struggles of other women, even women with whom they would ordinarily think they had nothing in common.

The responses here bear out two important truths that are woven into daily reality for all of us, men and women together; **1.** that for the most part, men in general are still coming from that "collective karma" (Welwood, 1990) of dominating women, even when they try – and many are trying – to change that for themselves personally. Whether it's a hierarchy of clergy or of husbands or friends or lovers, even men who deliberately cultivate their inner feminine, still carry the collective shaping of their gender. The change is very slow, and the evidence of the presence of domination often unconscious and automatic, causing it to leap out at women in surprising ways. The work of changing consciousness in this realm has really even hardly begun, and while women can do the work of their own individuation, they cannot do the work that men can only do for themselves.

2. that the power of women is growing with every woman who comes to the awareness of her own inner authority as highlighted in this paper. No woman of integrity wants to flip the dominance hierarchy, to take the place of men, of which – if we speak out at all - we are often accused. Rather, we know, we ***know*** that by being faithful to our inner authority we are already changing the world, and challenging the structures that have allowed greed, violence, fear and power-over to be the main qualities by which our materialistic Western society – the so-called "developed world" is identified. Bolen (2005, 18, 28) reminds us that

> when the agenda for the world is determined by men, it means that decisions and actions that affect the planet, and all life upon the earth are made by the gender that most likely does not know or care about what others are feeling, experiencing or suffering. Until women are really involved in what goes on in the world, essential information and crucial concerns are not brought to the table.

The dormant power of women together is the untapped resource needed by humanity and by the planet.

CHAPTER IX:
Living As If It All Mattered

It is not for us to prophesy the day (though the day will come) when we will once more be called so to utter the Word of God that the world will be changed and renewed by it. It will be a new language, perhaps quite non-religious, but liberating and redeeming – as was Jesus' language; it will shock people and yet overcome them by its power.
(Bonhoeffer, 1967, 63)

In previous chapters I have explored some specific realities in the lives of women, as well as large theoretical frameworks within which they might be more clearly perceived. As I begin to draw this book to a close, I want to ask the question "so what?" If we really took our own lives seriously from an inner view, and from valuing the uniquely personal differences among us, what would change and how could we bring about this change? What would a truly individuated collective of women look like? In this chapter I explore three areas of practice that could catalyze religious women –and really, all women - into taking a step onto the threshold, or even into, the transformative cocoon. *Secondly*, I highlight brief statements from the co-researchers' "tellings" that in themselves hold out implicative challenges. *Finally* I offer nine questions that arise out of the study and the dormancy it indicates we are moving into now. This image of dormancy and seed questions brings me full circle.

Practices That Catalyze Transformation

1. Critical Reflection In Community.

One of the most deadening qualities of present day communities of Catholic vowed women gleaned from my personal as well as professional experience is a lack of genuine curiosity and a general reluctance to question customs, authority, and the tradition of both Church and community. Questions are unwelcome, discouraged, and perceived as "negative." This quality is characteristic of hierarchy which operates on secrecy, witholding of information, and authoritative decision-making without consulting the one whom the decision most affects. These qualities today we would call "oppressive" (Chopp, 1995), yet many women's communities contain more than a trace of this old way of doing things, engendering fear-based, rather than egalitarian participation in community affairs.

The women who participated in this inquiry all found ways to keep their spirit of questioning, resistance, and inner authority alive. They echo the thousands of Catholic vowed women who have not spoken aloud their struggle, but who engage it daily with varying levels of awareness. Promoting a practice of critical theory as the operation of knowledge for deliberation of beliefs and activities in a community might increase awareness and provide a language for sharing it: As such, critical theories "seek to uncover illusions...[and] demonstrate how discourses construct regimes of domination" (Chopp, 1995, 79).

Introducing a practice of critical theory into such fixed communities fraught with the dangers of unconscious assumptions, projection, and exclusion would in itself require a tender sensitivity and compassion as well as long, faithful attention. It would involve, most of all, staying constantly present through the conflict that would inevitably arise. One way in which I see possibility for such conversations would be to learn and engage in Bohmian Dialogue (Bohm, 1996, 4) in the sense of "releasing a flow of meaning." The personal inner work necessary to participate in such dialogue requires suspension of both assumptions and judgment and a genuine openness to new insight, both from within oneself and within the group. Engaging in this level of listening and speaking would provide a container for the "difficult conversations" (Stone, Palton & Heen, 1999) to emerge. Kegan and Lahey (2001) also offer specific practices for preparing for dialogue. Baldwin (1994, 1998) in her Calling the Circle: The First and Future Culture presents what might be the most detailed and practical way for women to gather, since her work includes ritual and calling the Sacred into the circle process, as well as inviting shadow and projection into the group so that they may be brought to awareness..

2. Concourse, Rather than Discourse

Kremer (1992) suggests the limits of discourse - which "presumes a banished and unexplored other (eg., body, emotions, the feminine, wilderness, and the spiritual)" and offers instead a complementary model which he calls "concourse." For Kremer, concourse is

the expression of the story as a model of multi-dimension inquiry, in which all the formerly excluded dimensions are present...along with rational discourse, there needs to be ritual, silence, stories, spiritual practices, theater, dancing. (170)

Congregations of Catholic Vowed Women have been engaging for years in "rational discourse" in the multi-forms of planned renewal, especially when revising their Constitutions. There have even been attempts to introduce some of the other elements named by Kremer in his description, but these are all subject to the rational, and especially to linear time. Grieving "rituals," for example, are sometimes half-hour prayer services in which words are read from a prescribed form. Silence is short. Tears are often unseen, or embarrassing when seen. There is little room for deep, inner feeling, which is unpredictable and not bound by time. Nor is there space in such "rituals" for any expression of grief outside of what is planned beforehand. So there is no room for anything except the safe, controlled, prescribed expression of grief, which does not touch the depth of loss that has been and is still being experienced by Catholic women's communities. I suggest that the difference between ceremony and ritual pointed out by Somé (1998, 145) offers some explanation as to why the prayer services (called "rituals" by some) do not have their anticipated healing effect:

> From an indigenous point of view, *ceremonies* are events that are reproducible, predictable and controllable, while *ritual* call for spontaneous feeling and trust in the outcome. Whereas in ceremony there is a potential for boredom because the participants pretty much know what's going to happen, in ritual the soul and the human spirit get permission to express themselves...in a kind of unforeseeable yet orderly disorder. (italics my own)

It is this kind of ritual, an example of which is contained in Appendix C, called "Line of Fire," which might move Catholic vowed women another step towards the transformation that has already begun.

3. Transformative Quadrinity: Living by the Wheel's Wisdom.

My experience of building a Medicine Wheel and discovering the balance of "fours" described earlier led me to search further for a framework in which to know the meaning of my attraction. In doing so, I came upon the word "quaternity," used by Jung (1953/1979, 265) in his teaching that "wholeness in consciousness manifests in a fourfold structure." By the time of this discovery, I had coined the term "quadrinity" for myself, feeling my impulse to be an expansion of the theological term "trinity," which I had for a long time been perceiving as an incomplete symbol, without knowing why, and feeling vaguely heretical about it. In the now familiar intuitive way, I came upon the Merriam-Webster's Dictionary (1996) meaning for the word "quaternity" as "the union of four in one, as of four persons, analogous to the theological term trinity," but I decided to keep to "quadrinity" instead, as did my colleagues with whom the term was named and highlighted.

My backyard Medicine Wheel has become many different wheels in my movement towards balance. Wheels are about turning most of all, and flowing with that-which-turns, beyond merely human control. Neither can one walk the wheel the same way twice. The wheel has become for me a primary symbol of the Flow of Life, and I propose it here in a parallel sense of how it could be used for reflection in the life cycle of religious communities.

Figure 6: Transformative Quadrinity

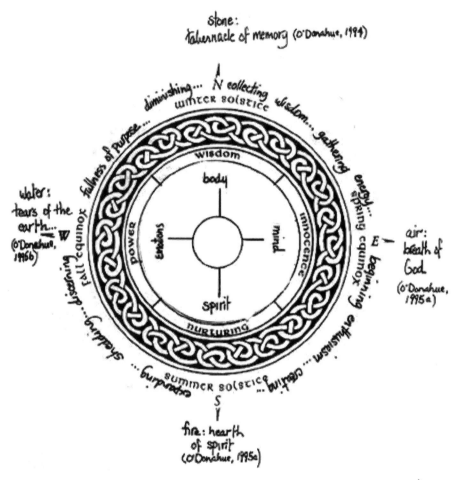

(Figure design by the author. Wheel by Davis and Leonard, 1996.)

Finding ourselves and our communities on the wheel in regular reflection might free us from the relentless pursuit of material performance and growth in numbers. It might bring us into the reality of the present moment and out of the prisons of past and future; thus making the reality of the present moment visible. Seeing ourselves in the great wheel of life, we might uncover our cyclical connection with the Feminine Energies of the Dark, of body and the flowing waters of emotion, which, along with mind and spirit, offer healing to an organic, evolving universe. The Wheel's Wisdom could re-connect us, not only with ourselves, but with the Divine, unfathomable Mystery whom we seem to seldom consider beyond lip service. We have lost sight of the reality that God is larger than Church, and that our faith is in God and life, not the Vatican hierarchy. The Wheel could bring us there, if we allow it.

Challenges of Storytellers

Earlier in this document I intimated that the stories shared by co-researchers indicate a hidden transformative power at work within communities of Catholic vowed women, one that found resonance with other women's struggles as in Chapter VIII. Indeed, these "tellings" clearly reveal a natural individuation process at work, even within the patriarchal systems of hierarchy. Though individuation has been confused with individualism in some writings on religious life (e.g. Leddy, 1990), the women speaking in this inquiry demonstrate the more advanced psychological functioning associated with the individuating process (Wong & McKeen, 1992) as "imagination, initiative, personal responsibility, integrity" (p. 19). These qualities illustrate the shift these women have made away from externally-referenced authority to an ability to speak and act from their own inner authority, acknowledging the lack of meaning that externally-imposed structures hold for them. They live by what Heron (1998) calls "spiritual discrimination" (198).

For these reasons, I highlight here some implications for the life of Catholic vowed women spoken by the ten storytellers. Here are their actual words.

157

We need to find out a lot more things for ourselves. (Grace)

We've been using feminist language but the structures aren't feminist. (Kate)

I lived with people who shared the same values, but it wasn't enough of the same values, and our group protest was pretty well lost. (Terra)

Grace...or passionate energy ...is always to move beyond what was. (Mary)

The more I became alienated from Church and...dead communities, the more on fire I became, being always on the edge of where most people were, in opposition to the norm. (Eagle Wing)

Reflecting on the vows has not helped me in my daily struggles. Despite the fact that I am able to do what is required, I am not energetically connected. (Sarah)

Part of me still hangs on to what could be because I tasted all that energy [after Vatican II]. Part of me still resists fully acknowledging that it's over. (Amy)"

The Church I live in is the Church of the People of God. And recently I've begun to think more that the Vatican has left the this Church. (Margaret)

Staying in the community while not being part of the institutional Church is standing in that paradox. (Cora)

I saw Chapters as...'mandatums' from Rome that are part of the oppressiveness that has kept us bound for centuries. I saw us as a group of women accepting this and affirming this oppressiveness by our own hierarchical system of dominance and inequality. (Grey Jay)

Reading these statements, I see circles of women sitting together in equal roles and entering into dialogue about the challenges these words present to the vowed life today. As demonstrated in the previous chapter, these circle dialogues would also be greatly enriched by the presence of women outside the lifestyle of Catholic vowed women.

Full Circle: Dormancy and Seeding

On a sunny October morning in 1998, I was turning the pages of my newspaper and came upon this headline: "Dormancy is Nature's Acid Test" (Oberdorf, 1998). Nothing I've written thus far illustrates chthonic/intuitive knowing as well as what followed. This title of a small essay in the "Gardens" section of the newspaper took on a numinosity and constellated a purpose which I've been following ever since. In that moment, I knew I had to look for a doctoral program in transformation, because only the discipline of such degree work would give me the tools necessary to write in acceptable ways, and I knew I had to write about what is happening in the lives of Catholic vowed women, with whom I was working almost exclusively at the time. This "knowing"was whole, instantaneous, and sustaining.

The organic image of "dormancy" has echoed through these intervening years. Just as absisci acid (which scientists identified only 30 years ago as the initiating agent of dormancy in plants) (Oberdorf, 1998) has an inhibitory effect on cell elongation, a similar agent is at work with religious communities in the developed world, canceling out the natural impulse to expand, and initiating what I believe to be a period of dormancy. Identifiable forms, by which women's vowed religious life has been so distinctly visible, have—like old seed pods— split open and fallen away. But the seeds are in danger of loss: neglected, even invisible, to those who keep trying to put the seed-pods back together, who confuse form with essence, outer with inner. My numinous encounter with "dormancy" all those years ago has led me to an even firmer conviction that our time and attention in religious life now need to be given to reflection, contemplation and critical discourse, letting go, inviting questions (with no answers), and attending to intuitive invention. What are the seeds we bring to dormancy? What is the essence of our values, emerging from our self-organizing, life experience? (O'Murchu, 2002, 51). Like the sap which nourishes the tree, we are already "in the night when the sap retreats, becomes denser and is drawn in the direction of the sinking sun and the root zone" (M. Karsh, 2000, personal communication).

But I am not the only writer to see "dormancy" as analogous to the present state of religious life. Wittberg (1991) writes an entire chapter on identifying signs of the death of religious life and suggesting activities proper to protecting and "re-sowing the seeds" (123) of core values in new, independent groups. Writing 12 years ago, Wittberg could not have foreseen the cultural effects of the internet and the growth of poverty and violence, but her suggestions for addressing the current dilemma are still applicable and would even be seen as quite radical by some communities. O'Murchu (1991, 1998, 1999) has also consistently held out for religious communities the necessity of "a paradigm shift of death-resurrection proportions for the vowed life" (p. 54), and he too recommends being "attuned to the seedlings of new life that the Creative Spirit begets amid the aridity and barrenness of this time of waiting" (54).

Echoing these two writers, I feel the pull of dormancy in my own late midlife and see it in the larger context of women's religious life, of which I am a part. The work of this inquiry has led me to see dormancy more clearly, however, and to resonate with it as

the death that is not death; but the initiatory death. The sleeping seed is mummified sealed in its shell, in its power of regeneration a living mortality. (Lawlor, 1991,136)

Most important, I have come to see that the *activities proper to dormancy*—dwelling with questions, without needing answers; attending to chthonic/intuitive knowing; releasing old forms; deepening presence through reflection and contemplation; surrendering to the chaotic darkness of creativity—as integrative, proactive, and integral responses to the liminal calling which has consistently characterized religious life in its original, fiery form. As a result, I suggest dormancy as a way to be in relationship with Estes's (1995) description of the life-force:

What is that which can never die? It is that faithful force that is born into us, that one that is greater than us, that calls new seed to the open and battered and barren places, so that we can be re-sown. It is this force, in its insistence, in its loyalty to us, in its love of us, in its most often mysterious ways, that is far greater, far more majestic, and far more ancient than any heretofore ever known. I am certain that in every fallow place, new life is waiting to be born anew (66-67).

Breaking Soil and Silence: Ten Seed Questions

The work so far thus concludes with ten questions. The questions here are a beginning: all who encounter these stories

161

and reflections will bring more questions, and someday the questions themselves might become answers. For a beginning, we can ask:

- *If "a belief in common values maintains coherence in community"(O'Sullivan, 1999), and this is not the present condition, what are our "connecting points" in the present time?*

- *Of what service to women, to the Church, to the meaning of community, to this social era and to our present historical moment are the stories told in this inquiry?*

- *If Catholic vowed women are moving to inner authority, why do we need the Vatican Church at all?*

- *What nourishes the authority of inner wisdom and what structure authorizes an outer one?*

- *What would organizations, including our own, look like were we to intend living by Wheel Wisdom instead of Map Progression for our practical choices?*

- *How can we recognize the individuating needs of women and create a container that recognizes the energy of the paradoxical link in our groups?*

- *How can we speak "the word we cannot yet speak?" (Morton, 1985)*

- *How can we live in the paradoxical link of inclusion and non-judgment, both within ourselves and within our groups?*

- *How and whom are we loving? How do we live by love in our days and in our years?*

- *How do we choose values based in feminine principles— including chthonic darkness—that are not gender-bound? How do we make feminine energy active in our daily interactions?*

In the spirit of this whole writing journey, I offer this fragment from Sarton's (1984, 21) poem, called

"Beyond the Question":

Can I weave a nest for silence
Weave it of listening,
Layer upon layer?

But first one must become small,
Nothing but a presence,
Attentive as a nesting bird,
Proffering no slightest wish
Toward anything that might happen
Or be given,
Only the warm, faithful waiting,
Contained in one's smallness.

Beyond the question, the silence.

For us, it is "before the answer, the silence."

In this way, and I would even say in this way alone, we might begin to glimpse a new frontier. Jesus was, after all, quite definitive when he said, "unless you become like little children, you will not enter the Kingdom" (Matthew 19:24). Like Sarton, he is here describing the interior disposition necessary for weaving the transformative cocoon.

CHAPTER X:
Spiritual Inquiry as a Way of Life: being a doorway

It is possible to prepare for the future without knowing what it will be. The primary way to prepare for the unknown is to attend to the quality of our relationships, to how well we know and trust one another. (Wheatley, 2002, 97)

The storytellers in this inquiry are questioners within a system that does not easily accept questions. Kate emphasizes this in her story about being elected Provincial, saying "no one asked anything important." If we want to change this way of being, we listen to our *own* questions, and allow those questions to directly affect our choices and actions. A willingness to question is the soul of liminality, concerned as liminality is with "the larger reality and the deeper causes" (O'Murchu, 1999, 19), and requires "fluidity and flexibility, creativity, and courageous abandonment to divine recklessness."(20) In this writing I have placed strong emphasis on the importance of recovering the personal, individual voices of women, especially Catholic vowed women, and this is where spiritual inquiry begins: with the one voice, the one question.

The aging populations of communities of Catholic vowed women occupy a unique position as our identifiable ways of life dissolves into history. Hillman (1999, 5) proposes "inquiry" as a focused intention for what he calls "the lasting life:" He quotes T.S. Eliot in saying "Old men [and presumably old women] ought to be explorers," and goes on to interpret this thought to mean "follow curiosity, inquire into important ideas, risk transgression". Coming to the end of this inquiry, I find myself initiated into seeing my own life unfolding as a "path of deep inquiry" (Macy & Rothberg, 1994, 29). Instead of ending something, however, I feel the beginning of a new way of life, the doorway to which is questions.

Pondering questions—and waiting for inner answers rather than thinking up answers—is a long spiritual tradition. Rothberg (1994, 3) defines "inquiry" as "a response to an existential or intellectual question through the search for insight, knowledge, or understanding". I wonder how it would be to pursue such understanding in circles of women who are willing to stay present to the pain, repressed feelings, and resistance to change that such questioning can bring? Contemplative Inquiry, using practices such as systematic contemplation, radical questioning, metaphysical thinking, critical deconstruction, and the cultivation of visions and dreams (Rothberg) might initiate and sustain those who are willing to step onto the threshold of, or even into, the transformative cocoon of religious life. These practices, all of which are congruent with Bohmian Dialogue, could be the ground in which the seed of religious life can lie dormant until such time as flowering begins another cycle. Committing to Baldwin's (1998) Circle Process over a long period could do the same. Practicing contemplative inquiry, either singly or in groups, could expand our awareness of the threshold moment we occupy in the history of religious life, might turn us into "Threshold People," might allow us to become "doors for others to walk through" (MacEowen, 2002, 13), people whom Somé (1998) speaks of as "a living doorway of Spirit" or Spangler (2001), translating John 14:6: "No man comes to the Father except through me," as "Through what I am, I open the door in each of you to the Sacred within."

Empersonal Spirit

Following cycles by walking the Wheel confronts us as much with what we don't know as what we know. Just as "knowing" creates a communion of knowers, so does inquiry create a communion of those who stay present to questions. Contemplative inquiry, drawing on and including what Spangler (2001) calls the "empersonal spirit" could actualize the long experiential wisdom of the collective of vowed women:

> In the alchemy of our everyday lives, we produce a spiritual quality that is expressed of a radiance born from the strength and power of our wholeness. It emerges from our personal effort to create unobstructedness and clarity within ourselves. It's the spiritual fruit of our personal histories and biographies. Its radiance may be weak or strong, but it's there in all of us. (97)

This collective "empersonal spirit" was present in the beginning of religious congregations, when those exploding, enthusiastic groups of women risked all they had to change their world for the better. Now, when age and diminishing numbers tempt us to despair, that spirit is still present, though in a different form, acting as concretely as "valences" (Flinders, 2002, 7), those bonds that connect particles to one another in a molecule, recognized by scientists in the structure of matter. Our common history and experience—and now our questions —

can today *more than vows* create "valences of communion" that consciously contribute to healing ourselves and the cosmos.

Alchemical Questions

What questions hold such alchemical properties?   Here is a beginning list. I encourage whoever reads this list to not only choose a few and carry them around like a talisman, but to add her or his own. In this way, we increase the radiance of empersonal spirit and our own original fire.

What do you think is the greatest problem facing us?

Do you think it's getting worse or better?

Do you think you can do anything about it?

Do you talk this problem with the people in your life?

What gives you hope?

When is the information about a given problem going to be sufficient.?

When is your experience of a given concern going to be sufficient?

What is to be done? What should I do? is it too late?

Why am I so uncomfortable with incompleteness ...lack of control...not always being right?

So what?

What is going on here?

What are you afraid of?

What do you love?

What's your deepest question?

What do you wish someone would ask you?

What seeds would you give your life to preserve?

Whom does it serve—that you stay too busy to think?

What is keeping this system going?

What are the dynamics of power in this situation?

What are you expected to believe?

How are you expected to consume?

Does it have to be like this?

How do I get out of here? (Questions adapted from Macy & Rothberg, 1994)

Each question is a tongue of fire. If we follow the questions deeply enough we will be transformed. And healed. And in our own healing, without trying at all, we will be the agents of healing the world.

CHAPTER XI:
Back to the Beginning:

LINE OF FIRE:

A RITUAL OF LAMENT AND RELEASE

I believe that one of the reasons why traditional communities of religious women in the Roman Catholic tradition have not been able to move unencumbered into the future is that what is lamentable about what we've lost has not been sufficiently grieved and released. There was much to celebrate in the old form of religious life, much that was hidden in the "Keep Out" structures that was a source of secret joy; I know that this was true for me, even at the age of seventeen. Unexpressed grief keeps the past present, though it might be buried as a weight that burdens steps forward.

This thought occurred to me when reflecting on Malidoma Somé's (1998) chapter on ritual in The Healing Wisdom of Africa, specifically, his distinction between ritual and ceremony. "Ceremony" is what religion in the West has become for communities: predictable, timebound, and unwelcoming of emotion, without which grief in particular cannot be experienced.

Many religious women's communities have held "grief rituals," but they are not rituals according to Some's definition. They are prayer-services (some not even ceremonies, which would include symbolic actions) read from distributed papers and completed in a half hour at the beginning or end of a meeting. Finished. Grief without tears, at least group tears.

I offer here a ritual design for religious women who know and can face that their life-form is dying. I make this statement in a general sense; it's the form, but not the essence, that's dying, and it's the form that needs grieving, or it cannot transform. I apply this only to the form of religious life of women in the West, those known as "active" communities.

It's important to note here that not all religious women believe this is happening, and that also hampers grief. Nor do all of them experience the kind of prayer-service I described above as superficial. My beliefs around this awareness have been growing for about 15 years, and they have taken firm root in my explorations of the deeper soul connections experienced in indigenous traditions. I believe in the necessary engagement of the powers beyond ourselves and the unpredictable outcome of such engagement as well as the grounding in our physical bodies and in nature for the depth of grief to have its full cleansing power. Only this quality of grief can be transformative.

I personally experience "being" as intense engagement with the world in all its aspects without judgment, and I continue to pursue this engagement in more and more direct encounters. I have found that when I cannot be present to myself, I cannot be present to anything, anyone else, and so I must practice being there. This presence has not been a lifelong habit, of circumstantial necessity.

My experience of being shapes my perception, and I have always experienced intellectual engagement alone as being narrow and constricted, always leaving me achingly hungry even while satisfying some important part of my brain. It doesn't touch my spirit, or it set off sparks of possibility that then fade into darkness for want of air and light. While achieving academically in school—I was simultaneously disdainful of the store that people seemed to place in top marks—as if they were everything. It was this "disdainful" feeling that was the trailhead of my search for the more, and I found it in parts of Buddhism as well as (mainly) in the earth-based spiritual beliefs and practices of First Nations peoples and the pre-Christian Celts. Thus, my ways of knowing deepened and broadened, and included the intellectual approach of the West, but only as a narrow doorway into what became for me "the real world."

LINE OF FIRE: the Ritual

This experience could take place from 10:00a.m. on a Saturday to Sunday at noon. Its setting would be in a place outside in nature, surrounded by trees, water, birds, animals, and the vociferous silence afforded only by such an environment. We would spend as much time in that outdoor environment as possible and have a large room necessary for the times we would be indoors, looking out onto this view.

There would be much fire present in the form of candles, firepots (the odorless, smokeless indoor flame made of epsom salts and rubbing alcohol that burns for hours), and outdoor fires as well.

The title of the ritual "Line of Fire" is meant to have a double meaning: As religious women, the ancestors of our chosen way of life show us that we come from a long line of fire through history's darkness. Many foundresses of our communities were rebels and scandals in their time, seeing what no one else could see and daring to bring it about against all institutional odds. This put them into the traditional meaning of "line of fire;" that is, "the front lines" of battle, and today we are trying to recover that first fiery impulse. Participating in this ritual is to step into the "line of fire" in both senses.

The ritual would have three parts:

- *Saturday:* Naming and spending time with some of the forms of the past (What did I love about it? How did it shape me? What do I really miss?). Bringing symbols of that past: parts of the religious habit, horariums, rosary beads, copies of "the rule." We would have a coffin-shaped box present into which we place each object lovingly, with respect and words of tribute as to what these objects did for us, gave us in times when women had no visible power, when—indeed— we didn't even know we were women.

- *Saturday, overnight*: Keeping vigil with the parts that still live in me, influence my thinking and decisions, especially in restrictive ways. During the night we would be writing, keeping the Great Silence (this used to be a part of our life together); listening for a new name which describes the purpose of life now; keeping an all-night vigil with the coffin; around 4:00a.m. opening a sharing of experiences including the assumptions and old beliefs that need transforming; finally, digging the hole and burying the old at dawn.

- *Sunday morning*: Greeting a new day, literally and figuratively: bathing, dressing in new clothes, proclaiming yourself the new name given you by the long night (a new name being a poignant echo of an old practice in this setting), having lots of flowers around, singing, telling stories of where you see "the new" already happening in how religious women are living; drumming and dancing, a celebration breakfast.

My Reality: Helping and Hindering

As I have already mentioned, not all members of women's religious communities believe that the form as we know it is ending, and to them, carrying through with this ritual would be in itself a scandal, an announcement of failure. It would be a move that would alienate many and throw a lifeline to a few.

My "reality," which gives priority to body, creative spirit, and nature experiences over intellectual conceptualizing—though including that also—would hinder a large number of women from participating in this ritual, especially those who could not tolerate the discomfort of unpredictable emotion and the lack of specific timeframes for prayers and other group activities. Those who need a dominant conceptual expression would also be uncomfortable here, and many would not even consider attending.

For those who would be willing to step out of their predictable frame of reference and into the unknown, this ritual would be a "disorienting dilemma" (Mezirow, 2000), lacking as it is in conceptual frameworks. The design deliberately gives conceptual reflection a very low profile because the group for whom it is intended has engaged in mostly that for much of their lives. Other factors that would possibly contribute to disorientation would be the primary presence of the outdoor setting, the coffin-shaped box, the all-night vigil and the new name. I am assuming here that these would evoke feelings of anxiety, fear, anger, loss, grief, even despair at levels previously unexperienced for many. The purpose of the 4:00 a.m. group dialogue would be to provide a container for whatever feelings have arisen during the night and to initiate a flow of communal meaning which would promote transformation of old beliefs and assumptions. It would also serve to promote the "recognition that one's process of transformation [is] shared" (Mezirow, 2000), which is crucial to the communal nature of grieving an organizational form.

175

One of the prominent themes of the <u>Bhagavad Gita</u> is detachment from the results of one's work. I would hope that an expanded awareness of the larger universal reality would be encountered throughout this ritual, especially in the dialogue on beliefs and assumptions.

Kegan (2000a) highlights the epistemological necessity of attending to two kinds of processes: "Meaning-forming; i.e., the activity by which we shape a coherent meaning out of the raw material of our outer and inner experiencing," and "reforming our meaning-forming; i.e., we change the very form by which we are making our meaning." The ritual I am proposing here would frame the possibility for just such twofold change. Not only would the understanding of religious life be experienced in a new ontological way, but the form by which we make meaning—true ritual in Somé's sense rather than by intellectual analysis and strategic planning—would also change.

Finally, I would place this ritual in the context of "the hero/ine's journey." The three parts of the ritual parallel the three "movements" of a hero-quest (Campbell, 1992, quoted in Ford, 1999):

- **a hero is called to venture forth from familiar lands into territory previously unknown**; in this ritual, acknowledging endings and letting go of the outcome of doing so comprises such a venturing forth, as would be the deliberate openness to the unknown.

- **the hero encounters marvelous forces and with magical assistance wins a decisive victory over hindering powers of the unknown;** this encounter is the purpose of the all-night vigil.

- **with boon in hand, the hero returns to the land of origin;** this movement is enacted in the burying of the coffin at dawn; receiving, proclaiming a new name, telling stories of "the new" already visible around us, so that we don't need to look ahead for the new, but only into the present moment.

It is my intention to create a "field of mutuality"(Gozawa, 2000) with this ritual, where different meaning perspectives characterizing the group would be welcomed and amplified with respect. Further, that surrender to this field intends to produce an experience of "inclusivity, love and grace" (Gozawa, 2000) flowing out of the ontologies of the good-hearted participants, and even more than that, out of the quality of Being engendered by the ritual itself.

EPILOGUE: WE ARE THE NEXT STORY

There is some talk in the various transforming communities about "being the new story", or about "telling a new story." Using such a term is a bit deceptive, not to say short-sighted. The unfolding will go on. The most we can say at this stage is that we are the *next* story, because what is unfolding in the large universe story surely does not end with us. Perhaps it is even more realistic to say that we are the *next chapter* in a story that has no end.

If this is true of the large view of the universe, so it is true of the smaller story of women in general and Catholic vowed women in particular. All the effort that goes into keeping things as they were, all the energy that goes into holding to a belief that we have to make everything continue as we were at the peak of our unfolding, is wasted energy and even more serious, it goes against the natural rhythm of creation. Choosing to take the step into the transformative cocoon – whether personally or communally – is to honor the creative vibrant Source that brings everything into creation and releases it back into the cycle, to emerge again, recognizable or not.

There is a mistaken belief among us that transformation is a grand and glorious change that will demand very little of us, because its result is positive and desired. This belief is so far from the truth as to be ludicrous. It can only be a belief of the intellect without considering what the body, spirit and emotions must go through in the transformative process. Neither does transformation take place all at once, some grand gesture that is dramatic and even recognizable, unless one happens to be the Beast in the musical stage play of "Beauty and the Beast", when – at the end – the Beast is raised into the air, spinning so fast we can't identify the moment when he becomes a handsome young man who is gently laid back on the earth again.

Transformation is more like a phrase from the theme song of that same musical: "just a little change" signals the beginning of transformation. Small, almost imperceptible shifts in how we perceive, what we see, what we are willing to question that we took for granted before. Spinning in the air – an image for being uprooted from familiar ways – can also be an experience of transformation but not necessarily and is only one phase if so. And we might go forward and back – trying to go back being a sign of the deep anxiety often accompanying transformation.

We are already transforming, though we might be at different stages, and with different questions. The new – or the next – is already here, happening every day as we read and research and try to go back and marvel at a new insight. Transformation has been happening while we try to understand it, identify it more clearly. How can we identify the new? They are often the ones on the fringes, the ones who ask frightening questions, the ones who shed old patterns and won't accept old answers very readily. They are the ones who step out of structures – not necessarily leaving them – but going far enough to both question them and to bring new thoughts back to old ways of doing.

Transformation – of the magnitude we are seeing in our lives today as women and as Catholic vowed women – can best be understood in metaphor, for we have no real language for what we are now experiencing. Nature's most powerful metaphor for transformation is that of moving from caterpillar to butterfly, but until the evolutionary biologist Elizabet Sahtouris told us the details, we could not make as accurate a comparison as we can now. Paraphrased in Korten's (2006, 74-75) writing, here is how transformation happens:

The caterpillar is a voracious consumer that devotes it life to gorging itself on nature's bounty. When it has had its fill, it fastens itself to a convenient twig and encloses itself in a chrysalis. Once snug inside, it undergoes a crisis as the structures of its cellular tissue begins to dissolve into an organic soup.

*Yet guided by some deep inner wisdom, a number of **organizer** cells begin to rush around gathering other cells to form **imaginal** buds, initially independent structures that begin to give form to the organs of the new creature. Correctly perceiving a threat to the old order, but misdiagnosing the source, the caterpillar's still intact immune system attributes the threat t the imaginal buds and attacks them as alien intruders.*

The imaginal buds prevail by linking up with one another in a cooperative effort that brings forth a new being of great beauty, wondrous possibilities, and little identifiable resemblance to its progenitor. In its rebirth, the monarch butterfly lives lightly on the earth, serves the regeneration of life as a pollinator, and migrates thousands of miles to experience life's possibilities in ways the earthbound caterpillar could not imagine.

Where do you see this happening now?

There is only this: we are already the next story. **Let the telling begin.**

REFERENCES

Aarons, M., & Loftus, J. (1998). *Unholy Trinity: the Vatican, the Nazis and the Swiss Banks.* London: St. Martins Press.

Allen, J. L. (2001). *Vatican Moves to Address Sex Abuse Problem.* National Catholic Reporter. Retrieved January 12, 2003, from the World Wide Web: http://www.natcath.com/NCR_Online/archives/120701/120701d.htm

Anderson, S. R., & Hopkins, P. (1992). *The Feminine Face of God: the Unfolding of the Sacred in Women.* New York: Bantam Doubleday-Dell.

Anderson, W. T. (1990). *Reality Isn't What It Used To Be.* San Francisco: Harper Inc.

Arrien, A. (1993). *The Fourfold Way: Walking the Paths of the Warrior, Teacher, Healer,_Visionary.* San Francisco: HarperSanFrancisco.

Bachofen, J. J. (1967). *Myth, Religion, and Mother Right* (R. Manheim, Trans., Vol. 84). Princeton, NJ: Princeton University Press.

The Bhagavad Gita. (E. Easwaran, Trans.)(1985). Tomales, CA: Nilgiri Press.

Bailie, G. (2001). *Violence Unveiled: Humanity at the Crossroads.* New York: Crossroads.

Baldwin, C. (1998) *Calling the Circle: The First and Future Culture.* New York: Bantam Books.

REFERENCES

_____(2005) *Storycatcher: Making Sense of Our Lives Through the Power and Practice of Story.* Novato, CA: New World Library.

Beijing Women's Conference. (1995) *Handouts for Participant Readings.* Beijing: United Nations Conference Proceedings.

Belenky, M. F., Clinchy, B. M., Goldberger, N. R., & Tarule, J. M. (1986). *Women's Ways of Knowing: the Development of Self, Voice and Mind* New York: Basic Books.

Belenky, M. F., & Stanton, A. V. (2000). Inequality, Development and Connected Knowing. In J. M. a. Associates (Ed.), *Learning as Transformation: Critical Perspectives on a Theory in Progress.* San Francisco: Jossey-Bass.

Bergeron, C., Y. (2002). Feminism and Religious Life: A Creative Fidelity. In G. Lussier (Ed.), *Religious Life in a Changing World.* Ottawa, Canada: Canadian Religious Conference (Theological Committee).

Bernard, J. (1981). *The Female World.* New York: The Free Press.

Berry, T. (1999). *The Great Work: Our Way into the Future.* New York: Random House.

Bohm, D. (1996). *On Dialogue.* London: Routledge.

Bolen, J.S (2005) *Urgent Message from Mother: Gather the Women and Save the World.* Boston: Conari Press.

Bonhoeffer, D. (1967). *Letters and Papers from Prison.* New York: MacMillan.

Bossy, J. (1985). *Christianity in the West 1400-1700.* New York: Oxford University Press.

Boston Globe Investigative Staff (Carol, M., Cullen, K., Farragher, T., Kurkjian, S., Paulson, M., Pfeiffer, S., Rezendes, M., & Robinson, W. (2002). *Betrayal: The Crisis in the Catholic_Church.* Boston: Little, Brown and Co.

Boyd, R. D. (1989). Facilitating Personal Transformation in Small Groups, part 1, *Small Group_Behaviour* (pp. 459-474)

Braud, W., & Anderson, R. (Eds.). (1998). *Transpersonal Research Methods for the Social_Sciences: Homoring Human Experience.* San Francisco: Sage Publishing.

Brookfield, S. D. (2000). Transformative Learning as Ideology Critique. In J. M. a. Associates (Ed.), *Learning as Transformation: Critical Perspectives on a Theory in Progress.* San Francisco: Jossey-Bass.

Brown, J., & Bohn, C.(1989). *Christianity, Patriarchy and Abuse: A Feminist Critique.* New York: Pilgrim Press.

Brown, R., Fitzmyer, J., & Murphy, R. (Eds.). (1990). *The New Jerome Biblical Commentary.* London: Continuum Publishing Group - Geoffrey Chapman.

Canadian Religious Conference. (2002) Unpublished statistics. Ottawa, Canada.

Catholic Information Network. (2003) *St. Angela Merici (1474-1540).* Retrieved May 6, 2003, from the World Wide Web: http://cin.org/saints/merici.html

REFERENCES

Chittester, J. (1986). *Winds of Change: Women Challenge the Church.* Kansas City, MO: Sheed and Ward.

_____ (1995). *Fire in These Ashes.* Kansas City, MO: Sheed and Ward.

_____ (2001). *Both Roots and Wings: Moving the Vatican II Church into a New_Millenium.* Paper presented at the Call to Action, Los Angeles, Philadeplhia, Chicago.

_____ (2003). *Scarred by Struggle, Transformed by Hope.* Grand Rapids, MI: William Eerdmans Publishing Co.

Chopp, R. S. (1995). *Saving Work: Feminist Practices of Theological Education.* Louisville, KY: Westminster John Knox Press.

Christ, C. (1995). *Diving Deep and Surfacing: Women Writers on the Spiritual Quest.* Boston: Beacon Press.

Clements, J., Ettling, D., Jenett, D., & Shields, L. (1999). *Organic Inquiry: If Research Were Sacred.* Palo Alto, CA: Serpentina.

Coles, R. (1989). *The Call of Stories: Teaching and the Moral Imagination.* Boston: Houghton Mifflin.

Congregation for the Doctrine of the Faith (2000). *Unitatis Redintegriatio.* Vatican City: L'Osservatore Romano.

Cozzens, D. (2000). *The Changing Face of the Priesthood.* St. Paul, MN: Liturgical Press.

_____ (2002). *Sacred Silence: Denial and Crisis in the Catholic Church.* St. Paul, MN: Liturgical Press.

Cranton, P. (1994). *Understanding and Promoting Transformative Learning: A Guide for Educators of Adults.* San Francisco: Jossey-Bass.

Crawford, T. (2003, February 1, 2003). The Veil of Silence. *Toronto Star,* pp. K1, K4.

Convict Creations. (2003). *Mary McKillop.* Retrieved May 6, 2003, 2003, from the World Wide Web: http://www.convictcreations.com/history/marymac.htm

Davis, E., & Leonard, C. (1996). *Women's Wheel of Life.* New York: Penguin Viking.

Ehrenreich, B. Great Women, Bad Times. *TIME* (1998, April 13) pp. 52-59.

Eisler, R. (1988). *The Chalice and the Blade: Our History, Our Future.* New York: Harper and Row.

Endean, P. (1996). Forward. *The Way, 36*(3), 173-176.

Estes, C. P. (1992). *Women Who Run With the Wolves.* New York: Ballantine Books.

Estes, C. P. (1995). *The Faithful Gardener.* San Francisco: HarperSanFrancisco.

Ettling, D. (1994). *A Phenomenological Study of the Creative Arts as a Pathway to Embodiment in the Personal Transformation Process of Nine Women.* Unpublished doctoral dissertation, Institute of Transpersonal Psychology, Palo Alto, CA.

_____(1998) "Levels of Listening" in W. Braud & R. Anderson (1998) *Transpersonal Research Methods for the*

Social Sciences: Honoring Human Experience. (pp. 176-178) Thousand Oaks, CA: Sage.

Evans, J. A. S., & Unger, R. W. (1992). *Studies in Medieval and Renaissance History.* New York: AMS Press.

Fallu, J. (2002) *unpublished statistics.* Ottawa, Canada: Canadian Religious Conference.

Fiand, B. (1990). *Living the Visions: Religious Vows in an Age of Change.* New York: Crossroads.

_____(1994). "Promises to Keep and Miles to Go". *Horizons* (Spring, 1994).

_____(1996). *Wrestling With God: Religious Life in Search of its Soul.* New York: Crossroads Publishing.

_____(2001). *Refocusing the Vision: Religious Life into the Future.* New York: Crossroads Publishing.

_____(2002). *In the Stillness You Will Know: Exploring the Paths of Our Ancient Belonging.* New York: Crossroad Publishing.

Flinders, C. L. (2002). *The Values of Belonging: Rediscovering Balance, Mutuality, Intuition and Wholeness in a Competitive World.* New York: HarperCollins.

Fox, M. (1991). *Creation Spirituality.* San Francisco: HarperSanFrancisco.

Frank, A. (1952). *Anne Frank: The Diary of a Young Girl* (B. M. Mooyaart-Doubleday, Trans.). New York: Pocketbooks.

Freire, P. (1970). *Pedagogy of the Oppressed.* New York: Seabury Press.

Fulkerson, M. M. (1994). *Changing the Subject: Women's Discourses and Feminist Theology.* Minneapolis, MN: Augsburg Fortress.

Gebara, I. (1999). *Longing For Running Water: Ecofeminism and Liberation.* Minneapolis, MN: Fortress Press.

_____ (2002). *Out of the Depths: Women's Experience of Evil and Salvation* (A. P. Ware, Trans.). Minneapolis, MN: Fortress Press.

Gilligan, C. (1982). *In a Different Voice.* Harvard, MS: Harvard University Press.

Goldberg, M. (1982). *Narrative and Theology: A Critical Introduction.* Nashville, TN: Abington Press.

Goldberger, N., Tarule, J., Clinchy, B., & Belenky, M. (1996). *Knowledge, Difference and_Power: essays inspired by Women's Ways of Knowing.* New York: Basic Books.

_____(1996). Cultural Imperatives and Diversity in Ways of Knowing. In N. Goldberger & J. Tarule & B. Clinchy & M. Belenky (Eds.), *Knowledge, Difference and_Power: essays inspired by Women's Ways of Knowing.* New York: Basic Books.

Gordon, M. (2002). Women of God [Online Journal]. *The Atlantic Monthly.* Retrieved January 20, 2002, 2002, from the World Wide Web: http://www.theatlantic.com/issues/2002/01/gordon.htm

Gozawa, J. (2000). *Cosmic Heroes and the Heart's Desire: Embracing Emotion and Conflict in_Transformative Learning.* Paper presented at the Challenges of Practice: Transformative Learning in Action, Columbia University, New York.

Grammick, J. (2000, September 16, 2000). *The Place of Silencing in the Teaching of the Church,* Conference proceedings, Haverford College, Philadeplhia, PA.

Grant, R. (1994). *Healing the Soul of the Church: Ministers Facing Their Own Childhood Abuse_and Trauma.* Burlingame, CA: Robert Grant.

Gray, J. (1995). *Neither Escaping Nor Exploiting Sex: Women's Celibacy.* Homebush, NSW, Australia: St. Paul's.

Griffin, S. (1978). *Woman and Nature: the Roaring Inside Her.* New York: HarperCollins.

Grollmes, E.E (ed.) (1967) *Vows But No Walls.* St. Louis, Mo: Herder Books.

Hall, M. P. (1977). *The Secret Teachings of All Ages.* Los Angeles: Philosophical Research Society.

Healey, K. (1973). *Frances Warde: American Founder of the Sisters of Mercy.* New York: The Seabury Press.

Heron, J. (1992) *Feeling and Personhood.* Thousand Oaks, CA: Sage.

_____(1998). *Sacred Science: Person-Centred Inquiry into the Spiritual and the Subtle.* Herefordshire, U.K.: PCCS Books.

_____(1999). *The Complete Facilitator's Handbook.* London: Kogan-Page Ltd.

Hildegard, Saint. (1995, 1986) *Hildegard von Bingen's Mystical Visions.* (Trans Bruce Hozeski). Santa Fe, N.M.: Bear and Co.

Hillgarth, J. N. (1969). *The Conversion of Western Europe 350-750.* Englewood Cliffs, NJ: Prentice-Hall.

Hillman, J. (1999). *The Force of Character and the Lasting Life.* New York: Random House.

Hoare, F. R. (Ed.). (1965). *The Western Fathers.* New York: Harper Torchbooks.

Hollis, J. (2003). *On This Journey We Call Our Life: Living the Questions.* Toronto, ON, Canada: Inner City Books.

hooks, b. (2000). *all about love: new visions.* New York: William Morrow and Co., Inc.

_____(2002). *Communion: the Female Search for Love.* New York: Harper Collins.

Hunt, M. (2002). *The Heart of the Matter: A Feminist Perspective.* Paper presented at the Regis College Symposium, Toronto, ON, Canada.

Institute of the Blessed Virgin Mary (2003). *Mary Ward.* Retrieved May 6, 2003, from the World Wide Web: http://www.ibvm.org/mary_ward.htm

Istrati-Mulhern, M. (1999) *Possibilities:* Art Cards. Goderich, ON Canada

REFERENCES

Jensen, D. (2000). *A Language Older Than Words*. New York: Context Books.

John XXIII. (1963). *Mater et Magistra* [internet site]. Vatican Press. Retrieved November 12, 2001, from the World Wide Web: http://www.vatican.va/holy_father/john_xxiii/encyclicals/documents/hf_j-xxiii_enc_11041963_pacem_en.html

Johnson, E. (1994). Between the Times:Religious Life and the Postmodern Experience of God. *Review for Religious, 53*(11), 24-33.

Jones, A. (2001). *Grammick: Silencing Inappropriate*. National Catholic Reporter. Retrieved March 4, 2003, from the World Wide Web: http://www.natcath.com/NCR_Online/archives/051801/051801j.htm

Jordan, M. D. (2000). *the silence of sodom: Homosexuality in Modern Catholicism*. Chicago: University of Chicago Press.

Jung, C. (1953-1979). *The Collected Works* (R. F. C. Hull, Trans.). Princeton, NJ: Princeton University Press.

Kaylin, L. (2000). *For the Love of God: The Faith and Future of the American Nun*. New York: HarperCollins.

Keen, S. (1983). *The Passionate Life: Stages of Loving*. New York: HarperCollins.

Kegan, R. (2000a). *Grabbing the Tiger by the Tail*. Retrieved January 9, 2003, from the World Wide Web: www.dialogonleadership.org/Kegan-1999.html

Kegan, R. (2000b). "What Form Transforms? A Constructive-Developmental Approach to Transformative Learning. In J. M. a. Associates (Ed.), *Learning as Transformation: Critical Perspectives on a Theory in Progress.* San Francisco: Jossey-Bass.

Kegan, R., & Lahey, L. (2001). *Seven Languages for Transformation: How the Way We Talk Can Change the Way We Work.* San Francisco: Jossey-Bass.

Kennedy, E. (2002). *The Unhealed Wound: the Church and Human Sexuality.* New York: St. Martins Press.

Kolb, D. (1983). *Experiential Learning: Experience as the Source of Learning and Development.* Des Moines, IA: Prentice-Hall.

Korten, D.C. (2006) *The Great Turning: from Empire to Earth Community.* San Francisco: Berrett-Kohler.

Kramer, H. (1973). *Malleus Maleficarum:on Witchcraft and Demonology* [audio-cassette]. Read by Ian Richardson. New York: Caedmon Audio Cassettes.

Kremer, J. (1992). "The Dark Night of the Scholar: reflections on culture and ways of knowing". *ReVision, 14* (Spring), 169-178.

Kung, H. (2003). *The Catholic Church: A Short History.* New York: Random House.

LaChapelle, D. (1988). *Sacred Land, Sacred Sex, Rapture of the Deep.* Silverton, CO: Finn Hill Arts.

Lawlor, R. (1991). *Voices of the First Day:Awakening in the Aboriginal Dreamtime.* Rochester, VT: Inner Traditions.

REFERENCES

Lawton, V. (January 6, 2003). Canada failing its women, U.N. says. *Toronto Star*, pp. A1, A25.

Leddy, M. J. (1990). *Reweaving Religious Life: Beyond the Liberal Model*. Mystic, CT: Twenty-Third Publications.

Loos, L. K. (1996). *Full Circle: Stories and Mirroring from the Matrix of Nature*. Palo Alto, CA: Institute of Transpersonal Psychology.

Lorde, A. (1984). *Sister Outsider: Essays and Speeches*. Freedom, CA: The Crossing Press.

MacEowen, F. (2002). *The Mist-Filled Path: Celtic Wisdom for Exiles, Wanderers and Seekers*. Novato, CA: New World Publishing.

_____(2007) *The Celtic Way of Seeing: Meditations on the Irish Spirit Wheel*. Novato, CA: New World Publishing.

Macy, J., & Rothberg, D. (1994). Asking to Awaken. *ReVision, 17*(2), 25-33.

Marion, J. (2000). *Putting on the Mind of Christ: the Inner Work of Christian Spirituality*. Charlottesville, VA: Hampton Roads Publishing Co.

Martin, M. (1981). *Decline and Fall of the Roman Church*. New York: Putnam, Inc.

McCoy, E. (1998). *Celtic Women's Spirituality*. St. Paul, MN: Llewellen Publications.

McInerny, R. (Ed.). (1999). *Thomas Aquinas: Selected Writings*. New York: Penguin.

McNamara, J. A. K. (1996). *Sisters in Arms: Catholic Nuns Through Two Millennia.* Cambridge, MA: Howard University Press.

Merriam-Webster's Collegiate Dictionary (10ᵗʰ ed). (1996). Springfield, MA: Merriam-Webster Inc.

Merkle, J. (1992). *Committed by Choice: Religious Life Today.* Collegeville, MN: The Liturgical Press.

Mezirow, J. (Ed.). (2000). *Learning as Transformation: Critical Perspectives on a Theory in_Progress.* San Francisco: Jossey-Bass.

Miller, J. B., M.D., & Stiver, I. P., Ph.D. (1997*). The Healing Connection: How Women Form Relationships in Therapy and in Life.* Boston: Beacon Press.

Mindell, A.(1985). *Working With the Dreaming Body.* Boston: Routledge and Kegan Paul plc.

_____(1993). *The Shaman's Body: A New Shamanism for Transforming Health,_Relationship and the Community.* San Francisco: HarperSan Francisco.

_____(1995). *Sitting in the Fire: Large Group Transformation using Conflict and_Diversity.* Portland, OR: Lao Tse Press.

_____(2002). *Working on Yourself Alone.* Portland, OR: Lao Tse Press.

Morin, E., & Kern, A. B. (1999). *Homeland Earth.* Cresskill, NJ: Hampton Press.

Morton, N. (1985). *The Journey is Home.* Boston: Beacon Press.

Murphy, S. (1983). *Mid-Life Wanderer: the Woman Religious in Mid-Life Transition.* Whitinsville, VA: Affirmation Books.

Murphy, M. (1997). *Women's priesthood? Few women agree.* National Catholic Reporter. Retrieved January 15, 2003, from the World Wide Web: http://www.natcath.com/NCR_Online/archives/013197/013197e.htm

Myss, C. (2001) *Sacred Contracts: Awakening Your Divine Potential.* New York: Harmony Books

Neander, A. (1993). *History of the Christian Religion During the First Three Centuries* (H. J. Rose, Trans., 5th ed.). San Diego: The Book Tree.

Nygren, D. and Uteritis, M.(1992) *The Future of Religious Orders in the United States.* Chicago: Center for Applied Social Research, DePaul University.

Oberdorf, C. (1998, October 17). Dormancy is Nature's Acid Test. *Toronto Star,* 7.

O'Donahue, J. (1994). *Stone as Tabernacle of Memory.* Inverin, Co.Galway, IE: Clodoiri Lurgan.

_____(1995a). *Air: the Breath of God.* Inverin, Co. Galway, IE: Clodoiri Lurgan.

_____(1995b). *Water:the Tears of the Earth.* Inverin, Co. Galway, IE: Clodoiri Lurgan.

_____(1995c). *Fire: At Home at the Hearth of Spirit.* Inverin, Co.Galway, IE: Clodoiri Lurgan.

Oliver, M. (1992). *New and Selected Poems.* Boston: Beacon Press.

O'Murchu, D. (1991). *Religious Life: A Prophetic Vision.* Notre Dame: Ave Maria Press.

_____(1998). *Reframing Religious Life.* London: The Guernsey Press.

_____(1999). *Poverty, Celibacy and Obedience: A Radical Option for Life.* New York: Crossroads Publishing.

_____(2000). *Religion in Exile: A Spiritual Homecoming.* New York: Crossroads Publishing.

_____(2002). *Evolutionary Faith: Rediscovering God in our Great Story.* New York: Orbis Books.

O'Neill, P. (2001). The Sangoma's Gift: Building Inclusion Through Honor, Respect, and Generosity of Spirit. In A. Arrien (Ed.), *Working Together: Diversity as Opportunity.* (pp. 203-209) San Francisco: Berret-Kohler.

O'Sullivan, E. (1999). *Transformative Learning: Educational Vision for the 21st Century.* Toronto, ON: University of Toronto Press.

Owen, H. (1992). *Open Space Technology: A User's Guide.* Potomac, Maryland: Abbott Publishing.

Owen, H. (1994). *The Millenium Organization.* Potomac, MD: Abbott Publishing.

Pagels, E. (1979). *The Gnostic Gospels.* New York: Random House.

Peddigrew, B. (2000) unpublished academic journal.

Peddigrew, B. (2001) unpublished Map of Religious Life, Past and Present.

Peddigrew, B. (2002). <u>Seed.</u> unpublished poem.

Perera, S.B. (1981) *Descent to the Goddess: A Way of Initiation for Women.* Toronto, ON, Canada: Inner City Books.

Plant, J. (Ed.). (1989). *Healing the Wounds: The Promise of Ecofeminism.* Toronto, ON, Canada: Between the Lines.

Ranke-Heinemann, U. (1990). *Eunuchs for the Kingdom of Heaven: Women, Sexuality and the_Catholic Church* (P. Heinegg, Trans.). New York: Doubleday.

Reagan, H. S. D. (1994). *Shamanic Wheels and Keys.* U.S.A.: Deer Tribe Metis Medicine Society.

Regan, J., & Keiss, I. (1988) *Tender Courage: A Reflection on the Life and Spirit of Catherine_McAuley, First Sister of Mercy.* Chicago: Franciscan Herald Press.

Reuther, R. (1975). *New Woman, New Earth: Sexist Ideologies and Human Liberation.* New York: Seabury Press.

Reuther, R. R. (2002, June 7, 2002). Abuse a Consequence of History Wrong Turn. *National Catholic Reporter.*

Rich, A. (1984). *The Fact of a Doorframe:Poems Selected and new 1950-1984.* New York: W.W. Norton and Co.

Rich, A. (2001). *Arts of the Possible:Essays and Conversations.* New York: W.W. Norton.

Rossetti, S. (1990). *Slayer of the Soul: Child Sexual Abuse and the Catholic Church.* Mystic, CN: Twenty-Third Publications.

Rothberg, D. (1994). Spiritual Inquiry. *ReVision, 17*(2), 2-12.

Rothluebber, F. B. (1994). *Nobody Owns Me: a Celibate Woman Discovers Her Sexual Power.* San Diego, CA: Luramedia.

Sams, J. (1999). *Dancing the Dream: the seven sacred paths of human transformation.* San Francisco: HarperSanFrancisco.

Sarton, M. (1984). *Letters from Maine: New Poems.* New York: W.W. Norton.

Schaeffer, P. (2000). *Gramick says no to Vatican silencing: expects dismissal.* National Catholic Reporter. Retrieved January 29, 2003, from the World Wide Web: http://www.natcath.com/NCR_Online/archives/061600/061600e.htm

Schneiders, S. (1991a). *Beyond Patching: Faith and Feminism in the Catholic Church.* Mahwah, NJ: Paulist Press.

_____(1991b). *The Revelatory Text.* San Francisco: HarperSanFrancisco.

_____(2000). *Finding the Treasure:Locating Catholic Religious Life in a New Ecclesial_and Cultural Context* (Vol. One). New York: Paulist Press.

_____(2001). *Selling All: Commitment, Consecrated Celibacy and Community in_Catholic Religious Life* (Vol. 2). New York: Paulist Press.

Seelaus, V. (1999). "The Self in Postmodern Thought: A Carmelite Response". *Review for_Religious_*(September/October), 455-469.

Senge, P., Kleiner, A., Roberts, C., Ross, R. B., & Smith, B. (1994). *The Fifth Discipline Fieldbook:Strategies and Tools for Building a Learning Organization.* New York: Bantam Doubleday Dell Publishing Group Inc.

Senge, P., Kleiner, A., Roberts, C., Ross, R. B., Roth, G., & Smith, B. (1999). *The Dance of Change: The Challenges of Sustaining Momentum in Learning Organizations.* New York: Currency-Doubleday Inc.

Shields, L. (1995). *The experience of beauty, body image and the feminine in three generations of mothers and daughters.* Unpublished doctoral dissertation. Palo Alto, CA.Institute of Transpersoanl Psychology.

Smith, K. K., & Berg, D. N. (1987). *Paradoxes of Group Life: Understanding Conflict, Paralysis and Movement in Group Dynamics.* San Francisco: Jossey-Bass.

Sipe, R. (1998). *Sex, Priests and Power: Anatomy of a Crisis.* New York: Brunner/Mazel Inc.

Somé, M. (1998). *The Healing Wisdom of Africa: Finding Life Purpose Through Nature, Ritual and Community.* New York: Jeremy P.Tarcher/Putnam.

Spangler, D. (2001). *Blessing: The Art and the Practice.* New York: Putnam.

Spretnak, C. (1991). *States of Grace: The Recovery of Meaning in the Postmodern Age.* New York: Harper Collins.

Starhawk. (1996). *Dreaming the Dark: Magic, Sex and Politics.* Boston: Beacon Press. Originally published in 1982.

Stevens, J. with Stevens, S.L. (2002). *The Power Path.* Novato, CA: New World Library.

Stone, D., Palton, B., & Heen, S. (1999). *Difficult Conversations: How to Discuss What Matters_Most.* New York: Penguin Putnam.

Stroup, G. W. (1981). *The Promise of Narrative Theology.* Atlanta: John Knox Press.

Sullivan, M.C. (1995) *Catherine McAuley and the Tradition of Mercy.* Dublin: Four Courts Press.

Sylvester, N. (2000). *Everything Before Us Brought Us to This Moment.* Paper presented at the LCWR Assembly, Denver, CO., 2000.

Taylor, E. (1998). The Theory and Practice of Transformative Learning: A Critical Review. *ERIC Clearinghouse on Adult, Career, and Vocational Education, Information Series_No.374.*

Taylor, S. M.(2007) *Green Sisters: A Spiritual Ecology.* Cambridge: Harvard University Press.

Torbet, W.R. (1991). *The Power of Balance: Transforming Self, Society, and Scientific Inquiry.* Newbury Park, CA: Sage.

United Nations. (2000). *Gender Equality, Development and Peace for the 21st Century.* Twenty-Third Special Session of the General Assembly. Retrieved 5/12/2003 from the World Wide Web: http://www.un.org/womenwatch/daw/followup/beijing+5.htm.

U. S. Bishops, Conference of (1921). <u>*The Baltimore Catechism.*</u> Baltimore: Benziger Brothers. Originally published in 1891.

Vatican II. (1965a). Decree on the Up-to-Date Renewal of Religious Life: Perfectae Caritatis (O. P. Austin Flannery, Trans.). In A. Flannery (Ed.), *Vatican II: The Conciliar and Post_Conciliar Documents* (611-706). Collegeville, MN: The Liturgical Press.

Vatican II (1965b). Pastoral Constitution on the Church in the Modern World: Gaudium et Spes (O. P. McNicholl, A. & S. O. P. Crowe, Trans.). In A. Flannery, (Ed.), *Vatican Council II: the Conciliar and Post Conciliar Documents* (903-1001). Collegeville, MN: The Liturgical Press.

Vickers, M. H. (2002). "Researchers as Storytellers:Writing on the Edge - and Without a Safety Net". *Qualitative Inquiry,* *8*(5), 608-621.

Waite, C. (1992). *History of the Christian Religion to the Year Two Hundred.* San Diego, CA: The Book Tree.

Walsh, M., & Davies, B. (Eds.). (1991). *Proclaiming Justice and Peace: Papal Documents from_Rerum Novarum through Centesimus Annus.* Mystic, CN: Twenty-Third Publications.

Ware, A. P. (1985). *Midwives of the Future: American Sisters Tell Their Story.* Kansas City: Leaven Press.

Weibe, R., & Johnson, Y. (2002). *Stolen Life: Journey of a Cree Woman.* Toronto: Vintage Canada.

Welch, S.D. (Ed.), *A Feminist Ethics of Risk.* Minneapolis: Fortress Press.

Welwood, J. (1990) *Journey of the Heart: Intimate Relationships and the Path of Love.* New York: Harper Collins

Wheatley, M. J. (1996, Spring). "Learning from Nature: Emergent Creativity. *Noetic Sciences Review.* (27-34)

_____2002). *Turning to One Another: simple conversations to restore hope to the future.* San Francisco: Berrett-Koehler.

Wilbur, K.(2000) *Integral Psychology: Consciousness, Spirit, Psychology and Therapy.* Boston: Shambhala.

Williams, J. G. (1991). *The Bible, Violence and the Sacred.* San Francisco: Harper Collins.

Wills, G. (2001). *Papal Sin: Structures of Deceit.* New York: Doubleday.

Winter Commission. (1990). *Report of the Archdiocesan Commission of Enquiry into the Sexual Abuse of Children by Members of the Clergy, volumes One and Two.* St. John's, NL: Roman Catholic Archdiocese of St. John's, NL.

Wittberg, P. (1991) *Creating a Future for Religious Life: A Sociological Perspective.* New Jersey: Paulist Press.

Wong, B., & McKeen, J. (1992). *A Manual for Life.* Gabriola Island, B.C.: P.D. Seminars.

Woodman, M. (1990). *Addiction and Sacred Emptiness* (2 audiotapes). Boulder, CO: Sounds True.

APPENDIX A: GLOSSARY OF TERMS

Rather than technical and formal definitions of these terms, I offer here the informal meanings of the words and phrases as they would be understood in the parlance of Catholic vowed women themselves.

Canon Law: the official law of the Catholic Church governing all aspects of Church life for members. Catholic vowed women were included in this law in 1901; prior to this date, only ordained clerics were so included.

Catholic Vowed Women: Also called "nuns," "sisters," "religious" or "religious women" (these words are often used interchangeably)—all these words refer to Catholic women who have publicly professed vows of celibacy, poverty and obedience within a particular Congregation or Order (see "vows" below).

Chapter: Originally a legally mandated meeting of clerics for the purpose of necessary business in governing churches, this word came into the language and experience of Catholic vowed women when they were included in Canon Law. "Chapters" are the regular (every 4 to 6 years) gatherings of Catholic vowed women in order to determine directions and decisions for the years until the next Chapter, and to elect leaders for that period of time.

Chapter of Faults: No longer used but mentioned in this book, this term refers to a monthly gathering of local communities of vowed women during which "faults" (not sins) were confessed aloud to the group and small punishments assigned by the superior of that community.

Congregation/Order: the term that describes the groupings of Catholic Vowed Women. Sometimes these words are interchangeable with one's "community," though "community" also refers to one's local community, or the women with whom one lives.

Dispensation: this word is used to delineate the process of being released (dispensed) from one's vows. After one has made perpetual vows, this dispensation must come from the Vatican itself (see "vows" below).

Ex Claustration: a Latin term for the period of "time out" requested when one is trying to discern whether to continue in the vowed life. While vows continue to define one's belonging to the Congregation, the time of ex claustration ("outside the cloister") is lived apart from one's community in order to help with the decision. A member may live in ex claustration for 1 to 3 years.

Horarium: the daily schedule of life for Catholic vowed women prior to Vatican Council II. Every hour was prescribed, usually in common except for ministries.

Ministry: refers to Catholic vowed women's work in the world; for example, "teaching is my ministry," or "pastoring a parish," lately one is also likely to hear that "massage therapy is my ministry" or "selling real estate is my ministry." This term describes an inner attitude towards one's work; that is, the sacredness of it, rather than the work itself, and is not to be confused with ordained ministry.

Mission, Vision, and Directional Statements: These concise and inclusive statements are written during Chapter meetings and represent that whole group's choices for involvement and action until the next Chapter. (See Appendix B).

Novitiate: the period of initiation into congregations of Catholic vowed women, usually 1 to 2 years.

Vows: As members of religious congregations or orders, Catholic women profess public vows (i.e., in a Church ceremony) of celibacy, poverty, and obedience. Immediately following Novitiate training, these vows are made temporarily for one year at a time (usually from 5 to 9 years) until the woman herself decides that she is ready to profess them perpetually (i.e., until death).

APPENDIX B: EXCERPTS FROM
CHAPTER STATEMENTS

The following excerpts from Chapter statements of a variety Catholic vowed women's communities in Canada, the U.S., and Ireland demonstrate an early emergence of transformative values some years before these values became common in our culture. They indicate beginnings of a "hidden transformation" of Catholic vowed women's communities within 20 years after Vatican Council II ended.

"Through all our ministries, old and new, we resolve to become agents of change in struggling to transform unjust structures..." (Sisters of St. Louis, Ireland, 1985)

"We claim our potential as Christian women by raising consciousness of oppressive structures in our congregation, our church, and society." (Sisters of St. Joseph of London, ON, Canada, 1987)

"We consciously choose to educate ourselves to the feminist perspective, and to operate from our understandings as they develop...we pledge ourselves to analyze, critique, and transform structures that keep the laity voiceless in the Church, and women in a state of oppression in both Church and society." (Sisters, Servants of Mary (IHM's), Monroe, MI, 1987)

"We, Sisters of Mercy of Newfoundland, are determined to collaborate with others as we commit ourselves to hold in trust the sacredness of all creation...we will empower ourselves and others so that together we can work to transform our world by confronting the injustices in Church and society." (Sisters of Mercy, NL, 1993)

"We, as members of the planetary community, recognize and respect the sacredness and interdependence of all creation. We are aware that when we lose the reverence for and awe of

creation as well as an understanding of our place as partners within the earth community, our sense of God and of ourselves is diminished." (IHM's, Monroe, MI, 1994)

"Living consciously requires becoming aware of the choices we make and the impact that these have on ourselves, others and Earth. We embrace the creative tensions that our diversity brings forth. We nurture consciousness from the deep wells of prayer, dreams, imagination, faith, and wisdom shared." (Wheaton Franciscans, Wheaton, IL, 2000)

APPENDIX C: MAP OF RELIGIOUS LIFE, PAST AND PRESENT

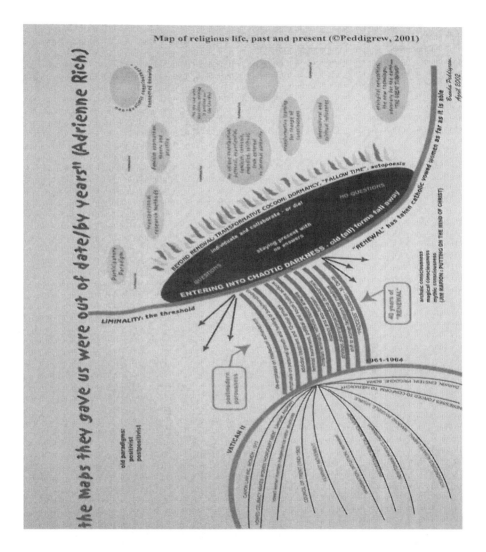

Map of religious life, past and present (©Peddigrew, 2001)

GRATITUDE AND APPRECIATION

My gratitude begins first of all my mother Anne Bursey Peddigrew, who taught me to read by the age of three, and thus opened the world for me even before I went to school. I thank those first Sisters of Mercy who taught me, lively young women who roller-skated in the gym and made fudge after school and showed movies on Fridays and gave me a sense of the vitality of a learning community in which art, poetry and music were as valuable as math and English. I am grateful for both the academic rigor and the deep spirituality with which I was welcomed and encouraged in those early school years. I felt at home there from the beginning.

I rejoice that I was young in religious life just after Vatican II, and able to plunge into the excitement and freedom and exploration that ensued. It was a great time to be alive, with encouraging Congregational leaders, and it gradually gave way to the deeper considerations, struggles and questioning that this book brings forth, and which are far from over. Along this engaging, vibrant way, many people emerge as I walk a line through my memories, people who in one way or another, and in ways they might not even be aware of, led to this book being written. I name them here in a litany of appreciation: Loretta Dower rsm, Mother M. Assumpta rsm, Sister Marie Michael Power rsm, Helen Harding rsm, Elizabeth Davis rsm, Patricia Maher rsm, Esther Dalton, rsm, Archbishop Alphonsus Penney, Phil Lewis, Gerard Whitty, Frank Ramsperger, SJ – shapers and supporters all.

Then a wider-spread community emerges: Marge Denis, Anne Kavanagh SSL, Margarita Synnott, Liz Campbell and the Grandmothers in the Arizona Desert, Allison Jensen, Rosalind MacVicar, Bethany and Joan Doyle, Veronica Dunne, Christina Cathro,

Christina Baldwin and Ann Linnea, Margaret Wheatley. The Wheaton Franciscans of Wheaton, IL with their special light, carried me through some doubtful times with their trust and encouragement of this work, especially Marge Zulaski, OSF and Gabriele Uhlein, OSF.

Of course nothing would be possible without the community of where one lives, both in geography and in the heart. The Writers' Resonance Circle and the Outloud Womyn's Voices of Haliburton County surround me with love and encouragement. My almost-daily phone conversations with Loretta Dower rsm, my Aunt Bride and my brother Keith – all in Newfoundland – keep me connected to the soil and spirit of my birth-land, and the sustaining power of family. Margo Ritchie csj (London) often infuses me with her own gentle questions and encouraging support.

And in this precious place of my writing, the property that has become known as SoulWinds, I am daily given grace and blessing by Joan Weir, Kai and MaChree, and the land that with them questions, challenges and comforts, again and again.

Brenda Peddigrew, rsm   SoulWinds, Halls Lake, ON, Canada
September 2008

26376197R00123

Made in the USA
Lexington, KY
29 September 2013